A New International Economic Order

Jyoti Shankar Singh

The Praeger Special Studies program—
utilizing the most modern and efficient book
production techniques and a selective
worldwide distribution network—makes
available to the academic, government, and
business communities significant, timely
research in U.S. and international economic, social, and political development.

A New International Economic Order

Toward a Fair Redistribution of the World's Resources

Praeger Publishers   New York   London

Library of Congress Cataloging in Publication Data

Singh, Jyoti Shankar, 1935-
  A new international economic order.

  (Praeger special studies in international economics
and development)
  Bibliography
  1. Economic history—1945-   2. Underdeveloped
areas. 3. International economic relations. I. Title.
HC59.S538   382.1   76-54508
ISBN 0-275-24170-X

PRAEGER PUBLISHERS
200 Park Avenue, New York, N.Y. 10017, U.S.A.

Published in the United States of America in 1977
by Praeger Publishers, Inc.

Printed in the United States of America

To
my children
Anil, Rajeev, and Ajit

Discussion of the New International Economic Order has dominated both international relations and the United Nations during the past few years. At first the very concept itself was vague. The poor countries knew that something new and different was needed, but they didn't know quite what. Then, as the dialogue between rich and poor progressed, the concept gradually took shape. In this book Jyoti Singh traces the evolution of the New International Economic Order (NIEO). He chronicles step by step the events that have begun to transform the idea into reality. Although this change is being described episodically in the daily news headlines, until now it has not been comprehensively described in book form. This is the gap which Jyoti Singh so admirably fills.

The emergence of the idea of a NIEO signals the end of one era and the beginning of another. It represents an effort by the preindustrial countries to gain some influence over world affairs and over the economic and other policies that directly affect them. They desire a more equitable world order, one in which they can participate as equals.

Since the beginning of the industrial era, if not since the age of exploration, political power in the world has been concentrated in those countries that controlled capital and technology. Historically, this political dominance took the form of colonial empires. The process of decolonization, which began two centuries ago with the American Revolution, moved slowly and reluctantly until the end of World War II. It has ended in a crescendo of independence movements. In the aftermath of World War II most of the former colonies achieved their independence. It did not take the former colonies long to realize that they had gained political but not economic independence. The old trade and investment ties still existed. Without economic independence, political independence was more form than substance.

A quarter century has passed since the postwar wave of decolonization. A new generation of leaders has emerged determined to create a new order. The countries they rule have the will and, more than ever before, the means to change global economic patterns. The concentration of political power in the countries that control capital and technology is diminishing.

As industrialized countries have exhausted their indigenous supplies of raw materials, they have become increasingly dependent on preindustrial countries. This dependence has been most evident in the case of energy. Because a disproportionately large share of the world's exportable energy supplies are located in preindustrial countries, these countries have new leverage in the international system. A few years ago the industrial countries of Europe, the United States, and Japan failed to come up with an effective collective response to the OPEC's decision to raise the price of oil. Their efforts to launch an effective energy conservation program, to develop alternative energy technologies, or to reverse the price increase were unsuccessful. Their collective failure revealed a profound change in the traditional power structure.

This changing economic relationship between those countries that control raw materials, principally energy fuels, and those that are dependent on imports of these raw materials has led to an upheaval in the world economy. The politics of resource scarcity has dominated international relations. For many countries, the terms of access to supplies of energy fuels and other raw materials have become even more important than the more traditional issue of access to markets.

The terminology designated by the international community, and used in this book (the New International Economic Order), suggests that the new order is an exclusively economic one. But make no mistake; it is not. In today's world economic and political power are inseparable.

The new order is many things. In the first instance, it is an altered perception of our contemporary world. It recognizes that the traditional one-way dependence of poor countries on rich ones is being replaced with global interdependence. It is no longer an "us and them" world; rather, it is "all of us together."

At another level, the NIEO is a set of rules that affect the myriad of relationships between the countries of an increasingly interdependent world. It is new voting rules for the International Monetary Fund. It is an effort to create an international food reserve system. It is a draft for an equitable law of the sea to govern the way in which the nations of the world utilize marine resources, both biological and mineral. It is weather-monitoring and information-sharing for the betterment of all mankind. It is efforts to control and stamp out diseases, to disseminate technology, and to stabilize world population. It is efforts to control inflation and reduce unemployment. The NIEO will, in short, determine the shape of the institutions through which countries work together.

In this book Jyoti Singh, writing from a vantage point within the United Nations system, describes with insight the historical transition from the old order to the new. We label it the New International Economic Order; but as I have indicated above, it is much more than a purely economic phenomenon. This transition to the new era is not yet complete, but it is well under way and, most importantly, there can be no turning back.

ACKNOWLEDGMENTS

A word of special gratitude to Rafael M. Salas, Executive Director of the UN Fund for Population Activities, for the generous encouragement he has given to me and everyone else on his staff to express themselves. Halvor Gille, C. Hart Schaaf, Erskine Childers, Tarzie Vittachi, Jay Long, Edward Trainer, and Bill Sharpless have read several drafts of the book and offered valuable comments. Lester Brown has offered several suggestions on the drafts, and kindly agreed to write the Foreword. I am deeply grateful to Marie Saldivar who patiently and accurately did all the typing. The views expressed in this book are those of the author and do not necessarily reflect the policies or directions of the United Nations or any of its member states.

CONTENTS

LIST OF TABLES AND FIGURES

LIST OF ABBREVIATIONS

AID	Agency for International Development (United States)
CGFPI	Consultative Group on Food Production and Investment
EEC	European Economic Community
FAO	Food and Agriculture Organization
GATT	General Agreement on Tariffs and Trade
GNP	Gross National Product
GSP	Generalized Scheme of Preferences
IBRD	International Bank for Reconstruction and Development
IDA	International Development Association
IFAD	International Fund for Agricultural Development
IFC	International Finance Corporation
ILO	International Labour Organization
IMF	International Monetary Fund
IRB	Industrial Resources Bank
ITO	International Trade Organization
LAES	Latin American Economic System
LDC	Least Developed Countries
MSA	Most Seriously Affected Countries
OAPEC	Organization of Arab Petroleum Exporting Countries
OAU	Organization of African Unity
OECD	Organization for Economic Cooperation and Development

OPEC	Organization of Petroleum Exporting Countries
SDR	Special Drawing Rights
UNCTAD	United Nations Conference on Trade and Development
UNDA	United Nations Development Authority
UNDP	United Nations Development Programme
UNEP	United Nations Environment Programme
UNFPA	United Nations Fund for Population Activities
UNICEF	United Nations Children's Fund
UNIDO	United Nations Industrial Development Organization
WEO	Western European and Other Countries
WFP	World Food Programme
WHO	World Health Organization

For three decades, development has been the major concern of most of the countries in Asia, Africa, and Latin America. As many of them became politically independent in the postwar period, their leaders were faced with the task of giving material substance to independence. The goals they set for themselves were expressed in quantitative economic terms, and were similar to those of the industrialized countries—rapid growth in gross national product (GNP), and expansion of exports.

The postwar period indeed saw a phenomenal increase in output and exports. The value of world trade doubled between 1950 and 1960, almost trebled between 1960 and 1970, and trebled again between 1970 and 1973. The major beneficiaries were, of course, the industrialized countries. The volume of their exports rose by 127 percent between 1960 and 1970, and by an additional 32 percent between 1970 and 1973. This increase was accomplished by the industrialized countries through use of cheap sources of energy and raw materials and through a spectacular breakthrough in technological developments.

The expansion in the exports of the developing countries was also impressive, though somewhat less dramatic. Their exports rose by 64 percent between 1960 and 1970, and by 18 percent between 1970 and 1973. As a group, they achieved an annual GNP growth rate of 5.5 percent between 1960 and 1970, well above the target of 5 percent set by the first UN Development Decade. Their growth between 1970 and 1973 maintained an accelerating pace, following the pattern of the industrialized countries.

These figures, however, do not tell the whole story. While 12 countries (for example, Brazil, Mexico, and Turkey) achieved high rates of growth, more than 90 other developing countries did not do as well. Those with under $200 per capita income registered the slowest growth in export volume, and the least developed among them actually showed a decline in export volume between

1970 and 1973. Accounts of aggregate performance thus hide the plight of those that were doing poorly or, indeed, very badly.

Let us look at another set of figures. During the first UN Development Decade (1960–1970), the gross world product increased by approximately $1 trillion. Eighty percent of this increase went to rich countries with an average per capita income of over $1,000 a year; only six percent went to poor countries with an average per capita income of less than $200 a year. The per capita income in some of the poor countries rose by only 1.5 percent annually during the decade. The late Tom M'boya, Kenya's brilliant economics minister, called it "the dollar-per-year Development Decade." We must also remember that per capita income figures hide the enormous differences between the rich and the poor in these countries.

Clearly, the economic and technological progress which brought such rich dividends to the industrialized countries in the postwar period did not enrich the lives of the people in the developing countries in any meaningful way.

It did stimulate, however, what is called a revolution of rising expectations. Free people in the poor world expect to get more out of their lives than their fathers and forefathers did; they are also unwilling to be as patient about their lot and to accept their poverty as the inevitable working out of their karma.

Coupled with this rise in impatience came the realization that the situation for many of the developing countries was actually getting worse as each year passed. Prices of manufactured goods from the industrialized countries continued to climb, while the prices of raw commodities from the developing world have been subject to erratic fluctuations, as shown in Table 1.

The prices of many raw commodities have also fallen in real value. In 1960, for example, a jeep cost the equivalent of 124 sacks of coffee to a Latin American buyer; today the cost is 344 sacks. In 1960, twenty-five tons of rubber could earn enough to buy six tractors; in 1975 it could buy only two tractors. Tanzanian President Julius Nyerere says, "When we were preparing our first five-year plan the price of sisal was £148 per ton. We felt that this price was not likely to continue, so we planned on the basis that we might average £95 per ton. In fact, the price dropped to less than £70 per ton."[1] These examples can be added to, both in terms of specific commodities or countries.

Eduardo Galleano, a Latin American writer says, "Our region continues to exist at the service of others' needs. It is a source of iron and meat, of copper and tin, of fruit and coffee; the raw materials and the foods destined for rich countries which profit more from consuming them than Latin America does from producing them."[2]

The exports of about 12 major commodities excluding oil account for about 80 percent of the total import earnings of the developing countries.

Table 1

Annual Average Market Prices for Selected Commodities, 1960-75

Year	Cocoa Indicator price Under ICA	Coffee Indicator Price Under ICA, all coffee	Sugar Indicator price Under ISA	Rubber Singapore No. I RSS	Sisal East African, UG	Copper LME	Tin Indicator price Under ITA
			Cents per lb.		$ per Metric Ton	£ per Metric Ton	Malaysian $ per picul
1960	26.72	33.80	3.12	35.4	255	242.1	393.7
1961	22.00	31.87	2.75	27.3	224	226.0	446.9
1962	20.81	31.09	2.83	25.6	250	230.3	447.8
1963	25.05	33.22	8.34	23.7	382	230.7	455.4
1964	22.85	43.51	5.77	22.3	369*	346.4	619.4
1965	16.57	41.02	2.08	22.9	222*	460.7	702.8
1966	23.48	39.61	1.81	21.4	209	546.0	645.2
1967	27.13	37.22	1.92	17.7	178	412.0	600.1
1968	32.70	37.36	1.90	17.3	161	517.0	565.5
1969	40.97	38.71	3.20	22.8	172	611.0	626.1
1970	30.57	50.52	3.68	18.5	152	589.0	665.0
1971	24.43	44.66	4.50	15.4	170	444.0	631.3
1972	29.15	50.34	7.27	15.0	240	428.0	626.6
1973	51.29	62.16	9.45	31.1	527	727.0	686.6
1974	70.77	67.96	26.66	34.0	1,056	878.0	1,133.8
1975b	56.51	71.73	20.43	25.9	619	557.0	963.9

*Estimated.

Source: UNCTAD, *Monthly Commodity Price Bulletin*, July 1975 (Special Supplement), January 1976.

3

Ultimately consumers pay over $200 billion for these commodities and their products, but the primary producers obtain only about $30 billion.

Even in the case of a commodity like oil, which has been in increasingly greater demand, it is interesting to note that its price has been subject to considerable fluctuation. The price of a barrel of crude oil, which was fixed by major oil companies at $2.17 in 1948, was gradually brought down by the companies to $1.80 in 1960 in order to sell more oil in the European and Japanese markets. The Organization of Petroleum Exporting Countries (OPEC) was originally organized by Iran, Iraq, Kuwait, Saudi Arabia, and Venezuela in 1960 to resist this kind of unilateral action by the major oil companies. Soon after its establishment, OPEC succeeded in putting an end to unilateral price determination by the operating companies. But as many of the producers were anxious to increase their exports, partly to offset the effects of price reduction and partly to obtain higher total revenues, they decided to offer 35- to 55-cent discounts per barrel below the posted price. This meant, in effect, a reduction in the sale price of oil. It was only in 1971 that the basic oil price was raised by OPEC countries to 1946 levels. Finally, there was the dramatic decision by the OPEC ministerial conference in 1973 to raise the price fourfold.

Fluctuations in the prices of raw commodities and the increasing amounts required for import of manufactured goods from industrialized countries have continued to affect the balance of payments of most of the developing countries.

This problem was expected to be partly solved by the provision of official aid by the industrialized countries to the developing countries. But this aid has never been able to fulfill more than a minute part of the requirements of the developing countries, and its percentage in terms of the GNP of the developed countries continues to fall. In 1970, the industrialized countries provided 0.52 percent of their GNP in aid. In 1970 the UN General Assembly called for this to be increased to 0.7 percent,* in the course of the Second Development Decade.[3] In 1975 it actually dropped to 0.3 percent and by 1980, according to World Bank projections of current trends, it will be 0.22 percent. Much bilateral aid is very often tied to purchases from the donor countries, and involves a relatively high expenditure on employment of foreign experts in the developing countries.

---

*The International Development Strategy for the Second Development Decade calls upon each developed country to provide a minimum net flow of financial resources (gross disbursements of grants, loans and direct and portfolio investment, less repayments of principal and disinvestment) amounting to 1 percent of its GNP to developing countries. Of the total, the strategy stipulates that more than two-thirds—0.7 percent of GNP—should be in the form of official development assistance.

As for loans, most of these were granted to developing countries on relatively hard, commercial terms; and with the passage of time, the debt burden has become so heavy that most of the aid received by developing countries is now preempted for debt servicing.

Under these circumstances, the gap between the rich and the poor nations continues to widen. There are many ways of measuring this gap, and comparisons of per capita incomes, as we have said before, provide a somewhat limited and distorted view. But these figures, imperfect as they are, tell a frightening story. Of the 4 billion people in the world today, 1.2 billion live in countries with per capita incomes of less than $200 a year. If we were to include China, the number would go up to 2 billion—half the world's population. As for the other half, about 1.2 to 1.4 billion live in countries with per capita between $200 and $2,000 a year, and about 600 million in countries with per capita incomes between $2,000 and $5,600 a year.

Within the developing world as a whole the gap between the rich and the poor has not narrowed appreciably in the last three decades; in many countries it has even widened. Abject poverty is the lot of millions of people today in the Third World. The average life span has been extended in the Third World countries, because of control of epidemics and major diseases and because of lowering of the infant mortality rate. But starvation, malnutrition, and disease still sap the life force and stunt the growth of millions of people. Lack of education, housing, and employment adds to the ever-increasing misery of these people.

The struggle to alleviate poverty is being fought at two levels today. Internationally, the Third World countries, represented by their elite, are pressing for changes in the international economic system so that they may have a more equitable share of the world's riches. Within their own boundaries, all of them, in varying degrees, face the task of using the additional resources they may acquire toward narrowing the gap between the rich and the poor. Many of them have already come to realize that western economic concepts and practices do not always provide the best guidance for achieving economic development and social justice in their own societies. Development is being defined, more and more frequently, in the context of the needs and requirements of an individual country or region; and qualitative standards, set in the context of the national or regional history and culture, are considered a more accurate indicator of development than an indicator based on GNP and per capita income measurements. There is also an increasing emphasis on self-reliant action to attack the problem of poverty without negating the value of international assistance and cooperation in specific instances.

There is thus a duality of approach on development issues. In the international arena, negotiations are still based on quantitative measures and goals; while at the national level, the discussion is increasingly about qualitative goals and self-reliant action to achieve those goals.

Most of this book is about international issues, and the action being undertaken to deal with these issues through international forums and international institutions. But a separate section is devoted to a discussion of issues and prospects relating to internal development and to the need for a new internal order to complement a new international economic order.

DEMAND FOR CHANGE

Let us now look at the history of efforts undertaken by the developing countries to bring about radical changes in the international economic order. Their demands for change were first voiced 20 years ago at the Afro-Asian Conference at Bandung (1955). Subsequently they were repeated and reiterated at the Non-Aligned Nations Conferences in Belgrade (1961), Cairo (1964), Lusaka (1970), and Algiers (1973); and also at the UN Conferences on Trade and Development in Geneva (1964), Delhi (1968), and Santiago (1972). In the organs of the UN and its specialized agencies, representatives of developing countries have consistently campaigned for equitable monetary and financial arrangements and for new institutional structures to help them in the development task. The establishment of the Expanded Programme of Technical Assistance (1949) and the Special Fund (1959) and, eventually, of the United Nations Development Programme (UNDP) (1965) were tiny steps in that direction. But no major changes were made where they mattered most—in the trade and aid policies of the industrialized countries, and in the international monetary and financial institutions such as the International Monetary Fund (IMF) and the World Bank, where industrialized countries have a controlling voice.

In mounting frustration and impatience, the Group of 77,* which first emerged as a bloc of developing countries at the United Nations Conference on Trade and Development (UNCTAD) in 1964, became more and more militant in its approach to international economic problems. With its majority in the United Nations and its specialized agencies, it was able to push through numerous resolutions stating and restating its grievances and frustrations. However, the single action that provided a dramatic manifestation of the economic bargaining power of at least a part of the developing world was the decision of OPEC to raise the oil prices. Western industrial countries were shown, for the first time ever, to be vulnerable to collective pressure from a group of developing countries. Interdependence no longer signified absolute dependence of the poor countries on the rich; the rich began to see how dependent they themselves are on the poor for many of their essential supplies.

---

*The Group now includes 114 developing countries.

It is important to note that the action by OPEC countries was taken not only on economic but also on political grounds. OPEC countries had long been dissatisfied with the percentage of oil income they were receiving for their own development, and were anxious to find some way of increasing their revenues. The political factor which heavily influenced them in October 1973 was the Yom Kippur war and the desire of the Arab countries involved to use oil as a political weapon.

Nadim Pachachi of Iraq, the former secretary general of OPEC, was the first to foresee the possibility of using oil as a political weapon and discussed the idea with his Arab colleagues. Prior to the Non-Aligned Conference in September 1973, President Sadat of Egypt also discussed this idea with government leaders during visits to several Arab capitals. Thus, when the opportunity arose in October 1973, Arab countries were ready, and took measures: (1) to cut oil production so as to reduce total available supply; (2) to impose, through the Organization of Arab Petroleum Exporting Countries (OAPEC), the Arab subgroup of OPEC, an embargo on oil export to countries considered unfriendly; and (3) to orchestrate the OPEC decision to quadruple oil prices.

The decision to raise oil prices immediately caused serious problems for the industrialized countries and many of them overreacted to the price increase when they forecast an imminent collapse of all the international monetary and financial arrangements. Inflation and recession increased but, clearly, the major sufferers were not so much the industrialized western countries and Japan, but the non-oil-producing countries in the developing world, which were much more vulnerable. Their fuel bills also went up astronomically, and as a result, both their agricultural and industrial production suffered heavily. Countries like India and Pakistan were forced to slash their development plans. Poorer countries like Bangladesh fared even worse.

Some western scholars wonder why the developing countries continue to support OPEC countries when they themselves have suffered so much in consequence of the OPEC action. The reason for this support, which does not seem to be slackening, can be summed up in one word—anticolonialism. Most of the developing countries share with the OPEC countries a colonial past, and the history of humiliations and privations suffered during this period is still vivid in their memory. Distortions in the current trade and aid patterns have not increased their confidence in the intentions or the actions of the industrialized countries. This anticolonial stance sometimes causes adoption of double standards by the developing countries, but it provides a logical explanation for the subordination of economic interests to political preoccupations by the developing countries.

The 28th General Assembly, which met in the autumn of 1973, provided an occasion for the developing countries to develop new initiatives aimed at seeking changes in international economic and financial arrangements. Algerian President Houari Boumedienne, speaking at the Algiers conference of the nonaligned countries, had called for bold new initiatives on development and international economic cooperation. The General Assembly decided in December 1973 to call a special session in 1975 to consider "new concepts and options (for) the solution of world economic problems, in particular those of developing countries (and) structural changes to make the UN System a more effective instrument."[4]

SIXTH SPECIAL SESSION

The monetary and energy crises that followed the OPEC action led to the convening, in the interim, of another special session on the problems of raw materials and development. The Sixth Special Session, which took place from April 9 to May 2, 1974, was the first special session of the General Assembly convened at the initiative of the Third World, and the first one that was not concerned with peace-keeping operations or related issues. On May 1, the session adopted a Declaration and Programme of Action on the Establishment of a New International Economic Order. (see Appendix A.) The declaration[5] began by stating its aim "to correct inequalities and redress existing injustices and ensure steadily accelerating economic development, peace and justice for present and future generations." The declaration, which incorporated a set of inherent principles stressing national sovereignty and equality of states, ended by stating that "the present Declaration shall be one of the most important bases of economic relations between all people of all nations."

The declaration emphasized the right of every state to full permanent sovereignty over its natural resources, and as a logical extension to this principle stated that "each state is entitled to exercise effective control over its natural resources and their exploitation, using means suitable to its own situation, including the right of nationalization or transfer of ownership to its nationals."

The Programme of Action[6] (see Appendix A) which accompanied the declaration proposed several urgent measures on raw materials and primary commodities, international monetary system and financing of development, industrialization, transfer of technology, transnational corporations, and promotion of cooperation among developing countries. The program also proposed emergency measures to mitigate the difficulties of the developing countries most seriously affected by economic crisis.

Expropriation of U.S. interests has long been a point of contention between the United States and several Third World countries, and the adoption of the principle of permanent national sovereignty over natural resources as part of the declaration was taken by the United States as the repudiation of a long cherished and well-established principle of international law. Yet, as Tom Farer points out:

The very fact that most Western scholars and diplomats speak of the obligation as if its existence were unquestioned is a sign of an earlier epoch's ethnocentrism. Latin American governments and scholars consistently urged the view that international law required nothing more than equality of treatment for indigenous and foreign investors. Yet, although they pushed all the right buttons on the international legal console and pedaled vigorously, they might as well have been silent for all the effect they had on the views expounded in Western universities and chancelleries or, for that matter, on the gunboats and marines dispatched periodically to enforce the law.[7]

The days of gunboat diplomacy are gone, and the threat of force is no longer a deterrent to confiscation or expropriation of foreign interests. What is effective is the threatened loss of private credit and private investment. That risk cannot be reduced or increased by formal changes in the legal standard long accepted by the Western world. Whatever the standard, private capital will not flow to countries that have shown undue eagerness for confiscation or expropriation.

The issue of compensation is, in any case, only marginally relevant to the question of distribution of wealth. The Third World must know this. The campaign waged for the change in the standard is therefore more of a defiant claim to autonomy than an actual anticipation of potential benefits to follow from confiscation or expropriation. Western countries, on the other hand, are equally concerned about the psychological effect such a change will have on their own standing.

When the Declaration and Programme of Action on the Establishment of a New International Economic Order was adopted by the 1974 General Assembly, strong reservations were expressed by the United States, Japan, and several members of the European Economic Community (EEC). U.S. Ambassador John Scali said it was "a significant political document, but it does not represent unanimity of opinion in this Assembly. To label some of these highly controversial conclusions as agreed is not only idle, it is self-deceiving."[8] The main objection was, of course, over the concept of permanent sovereignty over natural resources, because, according to the United States, the Federal Republic of Germany, and Japan, the declaration did not include the concomitant duty to pay compensation in accordance with international law. The declaration supported the concept of compensation paid in accordance with the laws of the nationalizing state.

While the need for transnational corporations to behave as good corporate citizens of host countries was generally accepted, reservations were expressed by several industrialized countries because the declaration did not call for the regulation and supervision of transnationals in a nondiscriminatory manner and in accordance with international law.

Some of the other industrialized countries did not show the same kind of resistance to the declaration and the proposed Programme of Action. Sweden, for instance, indicated that it regarded the program as an important general guideline, and its Ambassador Olaf Rydbeck declared, "for our part, we will from now on, in cooperation with all States Members of the United Nations, do our best to respond to it."[9] The representative of Finland said that some of the measures could pose problems for his country, but his government accepted and lent its full support to the documents adopted. In general, the Nordic countries showed a more outward-looking approach on the measures proposed by the developing countries, in comparison with the approach adopted by the United States, the United Kingdom, the Federal Republic of Germany, and Japan.

POSITION OF EUROPEAN SOCIALIST STATES

The position taken by the European socialist states provides an interesting variation. The involvement of these countries in international trade has increased in the last few years. However, the recent economic crisis caused by the oil price increase, inflation, and recession has not involved these countries as deeply as the market-economy countries and the developing countries.

Also, the amount of trade between the socialist states and developing countries is not very large. Of the total exports of the developing countries, 75 percent is absorbed by the Organization for Economic Cooperation and Development (OECD) countries, 20 percent is exchanged among the developing countries themselves, and 5 percent goes to socialist countries. This pattern is unlikely to change very much in the near future.

In the Sixth Special Session, the socialist states stressed the difference in the nature of economic relations between developing countries and the capitalist states on the one hand and the relations between developing countries and socialist states on the other. In their view, the capitalist states, given their past relationship with the developing countries, have a historical responsibility they can not avoid. Andrei Gromyko, the representative of the USSR, reiterated this view when he said:

> We shall never accept, either in theory or in practice, the fallacious concept of the division of the world into "poor" and "rich" countries, a concept which puts the Socialist States on the same footing as certain other States which extracted so much wealth from the countries which were under the colonial yoke. The authors of the concept are not only concealing the basic difference between socialism and imperialism, but at the same time are completely disregarding the question of how and at whose expense the high level of dependence was achieved.[10]

The socialist countries would like to see a link between disarmament and development, a pious but somewhat unrealistic hope. Stefan Olskowski, foreign minister of Poland, addressing the Sixth Special Session saw "the solution of the problems of international cooperation and of the problems of the developing countries in close inter-relation with the efforts of the United Nations toward detente, disarmament and international security."[11] Along the same line, Soviet Foreign Minister Gromyko told the General Assembly:

> Of late, the economic upheavals which many states have been going through have increased in intensity, and they are increasingly affecting the people's material situation. Statesmen and economists are racking their brains over the causes behind all this. But the conclusion that is borne out every day and every hour is beyond question: the aggravation of economic problems is largely connected with the rising scale of the arms race and with soaring military expenditure.[12]

The Soviet proposal is that the expenditure on armament by the five permanent members of the Security Council (the United States, the USSR, the United Kingdom, France, and China) be reduced initially by 10 percent, and part of the savings thus effected be devoted to development needs of the poor countries. This has been discussed in several organs of the UN and at several disarmament meetings, but nothing has yet come of it.

The role played by the socialist countries in the debate on a New International Economic Order has thus been somewhat passive, as they feel they do not have the same kind of moral and economic responsibility toward the developing countries as the Western industrialized countries. The socialist countries are also not members of OECD, the World Bank, or IMF, and have thus not been involved in the negotiations within these organizations on trade, aid, and development issues.

INTERDEPENDENCE

Though the attitudes and positions represented at the Sixth Special Session differed a great deal, one common thread that does run through all the presentations is the emphasis on interdependence. This is a recurring theme now in all international meetings and conferences dealing with economic questions. Interdependence is now defined not only as a strategy for prosperity, but also as a necessity for survival.

The concept of interdependence is in itself not new. Developing countries need the industrialized countries to purchase their raw materials and commodities, to sell them manufactured goods and products, and to provide them with development aid and assistance. The industrialized countries need, in turn, the raw materials and commodities from the developing countries to meet their economic and consumption needs. This relationship was, however, seen by the developing countries as being one-sided, in that decisions on prices and market conditions were almost always dictated by the needs and requirements of the industrialized countries.

What has changed now is the perception of the balance of power within the framework of interdependence. The dependency of developing countries on the industrialized countries has not decreased. But the industrialized countries have become much more conscious of their dependence on the developing countries for essential raw material supplies. European countries and Japan are, more than ever before, dependent on raw material inputs to maintain their economic well-being. Theoretically, the United States, if it tightened its belt, could survive without imports. But it has, so far, not demonstrated any serious intention to do this. Interdependence is thus becoming a two-way street. Whatever the rhetoric, both the industrialized and the developing countries seem to recognize this as a fact of life.

Confrontation has sometimes been advocated by individual countries or groups of countries as a way of ensuring their supplies. If the developed countries were to engage in a confrontation, they would end up paying higher prices for essential raw material supplies; exports of their manufactured products would decline; and their standards of living would go down. If the developing countries were to promote confrontation, the consequences may include defensive commodity stockpiling or development of substitute products by industrialized countries, greater support for protectionist policies in the industrialized world, a decline in bilateral and multilateral assistance, and a less significant role for international institutions and forums. None of these consequences is pleasant to contemplate nor very practical. Negotiations thus provide the only alternative to confrontation, and this became increasingly clear in the period following the Sixth Special Session.

This period—between the Sixth Special Session and the Seventh Special Session—was marked by several significant developments. We shall examine them at three levels—(1) the strategy adopted by the developing countries, (2) development of a response by the United States and the industrialized world, and (3) developments within international institutions.

Role of Developing Countries

The tone and attitude of the developing countries at the Sixth Special Session were stridently militant. This led to a series of confrontations, during and after the session, between the developing countries and the Western industrialized countries, particularly the United States. Militancy continued to be the norm in the public pronouncements made by the representatives of the developing countries after the Sixth Special Session. At the same time, they began exploring serious possibilities for negotiations with the industrialized countries. To this end, they joined with the industrialized countries and the socialist states in a unanimous resolution at the 29th General Assembly, on final instructions for preparing the Special Session on development and international cooperation.[13]

Working under the presidency of the energetic Algerian foreign minister, Abdelaziz Bouteflika, and at the urging of the developing countries, the 29th Session of the General Assembly also adopted the Charter of Economic Rights and Duties of States.[14] The charter sought to establish "generally accepted norms to govern international economic relations systematically" and to promote a New International Economic Order. Originally proposed by the president of Mexico, the charter was drafted over a 17-month period by a working group of 40 UN members under UNCTAD auspices.

The charter emphasized the right of states to nationalize, expropriate, and transfer the ownership of foreign property with "appropriate compensation" to be paid by a state according to "its relevant laws and regulations and all circumstances that the State considers pertinent." In cases where the question of compensation is controversial, "it shall be settled under the domestic law of the nationalizing state and by its tribunals," unless it is freely and mutually agreed that other peaceful means be sought.

In other forums, tough rhetoric continued to be exuded. At the United Nations Industrial Development Organization (UNIDO) Conference in Lima in March 1974, the Group of 77 pushed through strong statements on issues such as nationalization, export prices for products of developing countries, and commodity producer cartels. Similar sentiments were expressed at the Dakar Conference of 110 developing nations (February 4–8, 1975) and the Algiers Conference of OPEC countries (March 4–6, 1975).

The Arab-Israeli dispute continued to interact with the economic issues. The Arabs were interested in using international forums for criticizing Israel and for adoption of public positions against Israel. At the Organization of African Unity (OAU) Conference in Kampala and the Non-Aligned Conference in Lima, a strategy by the militant Arabs to seek support for exclusion of Israel was, however, modified, partially at the insistence of moderate Arab and African states, because of the fear that further steps in this direction would make it impossible for the United States to engage in negotiations on the economic issues.

The U.S. Position

At the time of the Sixth Special Session, the United States did not have a well-defined position on the issues raised. Its representatives defended the present economic order and refused to deal with any proposals for radical change. One of the reasons was that adoption of the Declaration and Programme of Action by the Sixth Special Session came at a time when major political changes were taking place in the United States, and the United States was simply not ready to formulate new initiatives. After the dust had settled in the United States on the changeover of administration, the State Department began to work on the U.S. responses to the developing countries. U.S. embassies were asked to make it clear to government leaders in the developing countries that exclusion of Israel from the UN would make it impossible for the United States to provide any concessions on the economic issues. "Give 'em hell" was the public stance assigned to the new U.S. ambassador Daniel P. Moynihan. This had had some effect as seen in the results of the OAU and the nonaligned meetings.

At another level, Secretary of State Henry Kissinger conceded that there were serious issues of a political nature which were entwined with the current economic issues in an inseparable manner. He first made this point at a speech in Kansas City in May 1975. The same month, he told the Ministerial Meeting of OECD in Paris:

> These issues go far beyond economic considerations. Economic stagnation breeds political instability. For the nations of the industrialized world, the economic crisis has posed a threat to much more than our national income. It has threatened the stability of our institutions and the fabric of our cooperation on the range of political and security problems. Governments can not act with assurance while their economies stagnate and they confront increasing domestic and international pressures over the distribution of economic benefit. In such conditions the ability to act with purpose—to address either our national or international problems—will falter.[15]

The Kissinger speech at the OECD ministerial meeting in Paris in May was followed in the United States by serious negotiations between the State and Treasury Departments on what the U.S. response ought to be to the proposals from the Group of 77. It was clear that without the support of the Treasury, Kissinger would not be able to announce an effective U.S. position at the forthcoming Seventh Special Session of the General Assembly; and Kissinger and his aides were anxious to promote a break-through at this Special Session, with the United States coming forward with several specific ideas and suggestions. Kissinger worked hard at getting the support of Treasury Secretary William Simon; this was not easy, as Treasury with its traditional belief in free market economics and liberal international trade has been opposed to such special concessions to developing countries as preferential trade agreements or price stabilization. Kissinger's speech at the Seventh Special Session, which apparently went through eight drafts, included a reference to Treasury Secretary Simon, indicating that the Treasury supported Kissinger proposals. This helped in greatly increasing the credibility of the Kissinger proposals.

Attempts were also made by U.S. officials, as well as many U.S. business and private groups, to draw attention to the plight of the non-oil-producing countries and the widening economic disparities among the developing countries themselves. This, however, did not succeed in dividing the Group of 77; if anything, it helped to consolidate the solidarity of the Third World. The failure of U.S. efforts in this area was vividly demonstrated at a meeting in Paris in April 1975. The president of France, Valery Giscard d'Estaing had proposed a conference of selected industrialized and developing countries, to negotiate on energy problems and related issues; and a meeting to prepare for this conference was convened in Paris in April 1975. This meeting was, however, unable to reach a consensus as OPEC countries, supported by other developing countries, refused to attend the proposed talks unless the energy problems were linked with raw materials and other development issues. The United States's efforts to restrict the proposed talks to energy problems were thus unsuccessful, and the scope of these talks was subsequently enlarged to include raw materials, as well as finance and development.

Response of Other Industrialized Countries

The United Kingdom seized upon the occasion of the Commonwealth Heads of States Conference in Kingston in April 1975 to float a new initiative on commodities.[16] Prime Minister Harold Wilson told the Conference:

> Everything that has happened in these past two or three years demonstrates the vested interest of all of us in a one-world system of commodity trade. ... We shall make no progress unless we recognize that large and sudden variations in price, not to mention uncertainty over supply and markets, are disadvantageous to both developed and developing countries alike. Both have a common interest in avoiding them.[17]

Wilson did not propose an across-the-board approach to commodity trade. "Each commodity," he said, "poses a special problem. Each commodity has its own elasticity of demand, its own production cycle, and its own special problems over storage." But he also emphasized that "those who are charged with negotiating arrangements for trade in a particular commodity can assuredly benefit from adopting a common approach based on mutual undertakings and relevant mechanisms."[18]

The Commonwealth Heads of Government agreed with Prime Minister Wilson's ideas and encouraged development of a common approach to commodity issues. Further evolution of the British position was linked with discussions and negotiations within the European Economic Community on a common approach to the problems of developing countries.

Along with the United States, France, and the United Kingdom, major European countries were also preparing to deal with the demands from the Third World. The EEC was engaged in trade and aid negotiations with a large number of developing countries in Africa, the Caribbean, and the Pacific, which finally led to the signing of the Lomé Convention. This convention, signed in February 1975, between the 9-member European Economic Community and 46 developing countries of Africa, the Caribbean, and the Pacific, provides these developing countries duty-free access to EEC markets on a nonreciprocal basis for all industrial products and almost all agricultural products. A fund totaling $3.6 billion was planned, to provide grants and loans over five years and to support a stabilization scheme to smooth out fluctuations in the foreign exchange earnings from a dozen main primary exports.

Following the signing of the Lomé Convention, there were intensive discussions among the members of the European Economic Community on the position they should adopt at the Seventh Special Session. The result was a jointly agreed-upon working paper which took a conciliatory position on debt servicing and stabilization of commodity prices and supported the idea of providing more aid.

Developments within International Institutions

Along with the evolution in the positions of the developed and developing countries, there were developments within the UN system itself, providing a solid framework for discussions at the Special Session. An international preparatory committee was appointed to plan the Special Session. The Economic and Social Council which met in July adopted a six-point agenda for the Special Session.[19] This was to include:

1. International trade
2. Monetary reform and transfer of real resources for financing development
3. Science and technology
4. Industrialization
5. Food and agriculture
6. Restructuring the UN system

In preparation for the Seventh Special Session, the UNCTAD Secretariat, as well as other concerned organs of the UN, produced several serious studies. One of the most thought-provoking documents[20] was produced by the Committee on Development Planning, which as a group of experts met in April 1975 to review the implementation of the International Development Strategy for the Second Development Decade and to relate it to the Programme of Action on the Establishment of a New International Economic Order (see Appendix A). Though disappointed with the results of the Second Development Decade at its midpoint, the committee saw the balance of the decade as a time of greatly improved opportunities for development, and called on the industrial countries to accept their continuing obligations to assist development and to see the gains vis-à-vis their own interdependency problems.

The committee touched on another aspect of the development debate—the need for a new internal economic order, to go along with a New International Economic Order. As the committee indicated, most of the dominant issues of development have to be thrashed out domestically. The debate on a new international economic order has centered so far on international arrangements and institutional structures. Any radical changes at the international level would not, however, be fully effective without radical economic and social transformation within national boundaries. Such transformation will require efforts aimed at spurring agriculture, broadening rural development, and mounting more effective direct attacks on the poverty and underemployment of weaker groups. International redistribution offers no painless substitutes for these required reforms. In most countries, in short, there is need for joining a new internal economic order to a New International Economic Order.

The World Food Conference in Rome in November 1974, which had been jointly sponsored by the United Nations and the Food and Agriculture Organization (FAO), had prepared the ground for a major discussion of the item relating to food and agriculture at the Special Session. Following the Rome conference, the UN General Assembly established the World Food Council as an interministerial body charged with the responsibility of regularly reviewing and coordinating policies concerning food production, nutrition, food security, food trade, and food aid. As a follow-up to another recommendation of the Rome conference, the establishment of an International Fund for Agricultural Development (IFAD) was discussed at a meeting of interested countries in Geneva on May 5–6, 1975.

Discussions within the International Monetary Fund and the World Bank which were scheduled for September were to deal with monetary and financial questions at the same time as the Special Session.

As for the restructuring of the United Nations, a committee of experts appointed at the instance of the General Assembly had prepared and submitted a report containing "proposals on structural changes . . . which could lead to an expanded role for the United Nations system in economic and social development."[21]

The stage was thus set for a serious and constructive discussion at the Seventh Special Session on a wide range of topics concerning the international economic situation and institutional responses needed to deal with this situation. The politics of confrontation so evident at the Sixth Special Session and also to some extent at the 29th General Assembly were to be replaced by the politics of conciliation. Delegations went into the Seventh Special Session with hope; though this hope was tempered by the realization that the changes that the developing countries were seeking would not be easy to negotiate, whatever the amount of goodwill and the willingness to discuss issues that characterized the mood at the start of the Seventh Session.

NOTES

1. *The New Internationalist,* October 1975, pp. 13–14.
2. Ibid., p. 14.
3. United Nations, General Assembly, *Resolution 2625* (XXV), October 24, 1970.
4. United Nations, General Assembly, *Resolution 3172* (XXVIII), December 17, 1973.
5. United Nations, General Assembly, *Resolution 3201* (S-VI), May 1, 1974.
6. United Nations, General Assembly, *Resolution 3202* (S-VI), May 1, 1974.
7. Tom Farer, "The U.S. and the Third World: The Basis for Accommodation," *Foreign Affairs,* October 1975, pp. 83–84.
8. United Nations, General Assembly, Sixth Special Session, *Official Records, 2229th Plenary Meeting,* 1974, p. 7.
9. Ibid., p. 11.
10. United Nations, General Assembly, Sixth Special Session, *Official Records, 2210th Meeting,* 1974, p. 9.
11. United Nations, General Assembly, Sixth Special Session, *Official Records, 2224th Meeting,* 1974, p. 4.
12. United Nations, General Assembly, Seventh Special Session, *Issues and Background* (New York, 1975), p. 13.
13. United Nations, General Assembly, *Resolution 3343* (XXIX), December 17, 1974.
14. United Nations, General Assembly, *Resolution 3281* (XXIX), December 12, 1974.
15. United Nations, General Assembly, Seventh Special Session, *Issues and Background,* op. cit., p. 16.
16. *World Economic Interdependence and Trade in Commodities,* Command 6067, London, HMSO, 1975.
17. United Nations, General Assembly, Seventh Special Session, *Issues and Background,* op. cit., p. 20.
18. Ibid., pp. 20–21.
19. United Nations, ECOSOC *Resolution 1980* (LIX), July 31, 1975.
20. United Nations, doc. E5671, May 1975.
21. *A New United Nations Structure for Global Economic Cooperation,* UN Sales No. E 7511 A.F., 1975.

CHAPTER

2

THE SEVENTH
SPECIAL SESSION

Perhaps never before in the history of the United Nations has there been so intensive and so genuine a negotiation between so many nations on so profoundly important a range of issues. We have shown that we can negotiate in good faith and doing so, reach genuine accord. Not least we have shown that this can be done in the unique and indispensable setting of the United Nations.[1]

U.S. Ambassador Daniel P. Moynihan, who spoke these words at the end of the Seventh Special Session, was expressing the views of many at the outcome of the session.

A somewhat more cautious assessment came from Pakistan Ambassador Iqbal Akhund, who had played a crucial role in the negotiations at the session. "I would not describe the present feeling as euphoria by any means. There is a very realistic appreciation among all of us of what has been achieved, and how much more needs to be done."[2]

These two views sum up in a way the Seventh Special Session. The session's great achievement was that it opened up the channels of communication between the industrialized and the developing countries, channels that had been clogged because of mutual suspicion and recrimination. On most substantive issues, however, it only registered and reflected the actual state of affairs, and pointed out the need for further discussions and further negotiations.

The Seventh Special Session of the United Nations General Assembly which began on Monday, September 1, was set to end on September 12, but had to be extended until September 16. Its results were incorporated in a final resolution entitled "Development and International Economic Cooperation" (see Appendix B).

The work of the Special Session was planned by an intergovernmental preparatory committee, which had met three times before the session. The general outline of the resolution adopted by the Seventh Special Session is based on the framework proposed by the preparatory committee, which in turn was based on the agenda proposed by the Economic and Social Council meeting in Geneva in July.

The preparatory committee made a major recommendation on the structure of the assembly itself, which in a sense profoundly affected the result of the session.[3] The committee recommended that while the general debate on the theme of the Special Session would take place in the plenary, detailed consideration of proposals relating to Item 7 of the provisional agenda—Development and International Economic Cooperation (see Appendix B)—should be entrusted to an ad hoc committee. Thus, while representatives of member governments presented formal statements at the plenary, the ad hoc committee meeting in the basement, directly under the assembly floor, grappled with all the difficult and delicate issues requiring negotiations. The ad hoc committee, which was composed of the entire membership of the assembly, was itself authorized to set up working groups as necessary, and did indeed set up two major working groups—one to deal with international trade and transfer of resources and the other to deal with science and technology, industrialization, food and agriculture, and restructuring of the economic and social sectors of the UN. Several informal meetings also took place, sometimes late into the night, to work on delicate problems.

The Plenary Session opened with addresses by the foreign minister of Algeria, Abdelaziz Bouteflika, and UN Secretary General, Kurt Waldheim. Bouteflika, as the president of the 29th Session of the General Assembly, was elected to preside over the Seventh Special Session as well.[4]

The speech by Bouteflika[5] was a mixture of militant rhetoric and conciliatory words. He categorically asserted "that the prosperity of the West is derived, to a large extent from the draining the wealth and exploitation of the labour of the peoples of the Third World, and that their economic apparatus, imposing though it be, rests on fragile and vulnerable foundations."[6] He went on to say that "at a time when the complexity of the world economy stresses the interdependence of states, it is no longer possible for anyone to impose solutions of his choice."[7]

Clarifying the position of the developing countries, he said that "it is no part of the intentions of the Third World, regardless of what is said of us, to impose solutions on anyone. To do so would not be consistent with either the realism of the developing countries or the purposes of this Organization."[8]

He added that "this session must . . . blaze the trail for this long process of restructuring the world economy by, first, adopting practical measures to solve one series of priority problems and, secondly, establishing the framework and objectives of subsequent negotiations."[9]

Bouteflika also referred to the Declaration and Programme of Action for the Establishment of a New International Economic Order (see Appendix A) and the Charter of the Economic Rights and Duties of States and linked the preparatory meetings of OPEC and the nonaligned countries as well as the UN Conferences on Food, Population, and Industrialization to the moves toward the establishment of a new international economic order. The lead he thus gave for a broader discussion of the interrelated issues of development was, however, not picked up by the delegates, who decided to focus on the questions of raw materials, energy, food, finance, and development, leaving out such contemporary and related issues as environment, population, and women.

In his speech, Kurt Waldheim, the UN secretary general, referred to the preparatory activities that had preceded the Special Session.[10] These included the Foreign Ministers' Conference of the Non-Aligned Countries in Lima, the Dakar Conference on Raw Materials, the Meeting of Commonwealth Heads in April, the meeting of OECD Ministers in May, the negotiations leading to the Lomé Convention, as well as intensive discussions within governments.

The secretary general naturally emphasized the hope that the United Nations would play a central role in the continuing negotiations on changes in the international economic order and referred to three functions that he felt the United Nations

> ... should perform in the mix of interacting events that are organized within and outside the United Nations System.
>
> First, through this Assembly, the United Nations should provide the blueprint, framework and guidelines for the negotiating process which will ensue both within and outside the United Nations System.
>
> Second, the results of these negotiations should be brought before the General Assembly in order to give such agreements the confirmation which only a universal organization can provide.
>
> Finally, the United Nations is particularly suited to providing continuity by monitoring and following up agreements reached by the international community.[11]

Both Bouteflika and Waldheim emphasized the importance of the forthcoming Paris talks on energy, raw materials, finance, and development, and the secretary general underlined the need to define the relationship of the Paris meeting and the subsequent negotiations with the United Nations.

The general debate in the plenary sessions that followed these two opening speeches lasted ten days and 22 plenary meetings. The topics touched on in these statements related to the six major areas of concern put on the agenda of the Special Session by the Economic and Social Council. Restructuring of the UN system, one of the six topics, was, however, not mentioned in many statements.

At the Economic and Social Council session in July, as well as at the preparatory committee meetings, the Group of 77 had given indications that it would like to see the question of restructuring taken up only after substantive policy issues had been thrashed out. This view also prevailed at the Special Session, where most delegations felt that restructuring would be better covered in the regular General Assembly, and that in any case, consideration of this topic could wait till the major global issues relating to trade, aid, and development had been dealt with.

The points of view presented in the general debate may be broadly grouped as those of (1) developing countries, (2) developed countries, and (3) socialist countries.

CASE FOR THE POOR

The first speaker in the general debate was Antonio F. Azeredo Da Silveira, the Brazilian minister for external relations, who referred to two levels of relationships that existed in the international economic field:[12]

> At one level, that of the economic relations among industrialized countries, there exists a relatively effective framework of rules capable of disciplining over-all developments with a view towards that harmonious development which the majority of these countries are already achieving internally, thanks to the action of their governments. At another level, relations between developed and developing countries take place—and there a virtual laissez-faire prevails.[13]

In his view, the trading and financial systems established in Havana and at Bretton Woods in practice essentially reflect the interest and peculiarities of the advanced economies. "The economic relations between developed and developing countries were never the object of specific rules which would reflect their particular socioeconomic conditions."[14]

Azeredo Da Silveira called for negotiations on a general agreement on trade between developed and developing countries, and concluded on a hopeful note by saying that "for the first time—and this is a positive consequence of the energy crisis—developed and developing countries are in a position to negotiate effectively and to offer equivalent concessions."[15]

Manuel Perez Guerrero, minister of state for international economic affairs of Venezuela defended, as a member of OPEC, the OPEC decision to quadruple oil prices but also emphasized the need for a dialogue rather than a confrontation.[16] Referring to the proposed Paris talks, he said, "We have not been motivated by a desire for confrontation. Rather, we wish to seek the bases of an understanding that will take into account the interest of all the parties."[17]

M. Jamshed Amouzegar, the minister of interior of Iran, also defended the OPEC action.[18] He pointed out that "by a curious logic, the fixing of oil prices by the major oil companies in the past was not considered a cartel action, and yet today the setting of prices by oil-producing nations in the exercise of their sovereign rights is so harshly criticized."[19]

Y. B. Chavan, foreign minister of India, touched on two main aspects of international cooperation for development and trade.[20] "Not only have the targets for aid set in the International Development Strategy not been reached, but there has been a gradual contraction in real terms."[21] As for trade, Chavan pointed out that the prices of most commodities exported by developing countries remain either depressed or unstable. "The import bills of most developing countries have increased to such an extent that even with a 100 percent increase in export earnings, there is no assurance that the imbalance will be corrected or even met halfway."[22]

CASE FOR THE RICH

On the side of the developed countries, the major statement was made by Ambassador Daniel P. Moynihan, on behalf of U.S. Secretary of State Kissinger, who was busy with the Middle-East negotiations and could not attend the Special Session.[23] The statement, which—unexpectedly for many—was conciliatory in tone, emphasized that

> ... there must be consensus, first and foremost, on the principle that our common development goals can be achieved only by cooperation, not by the politics of confrontation. There must be consensus that acknowledges our respective concerns and our mutual responsibilities. The consensus must embrace the broadest possible participation in international decisions. The developing countries must have a role and voice in the international system, especially in decisions that affect them. But those nations who are asked to provide resources and effort to carry out the decisions must be accorded a commensurate voice.[24]

Moynihan said further:

> An effective development strategy should concentrate on five fundamental areas: First we must apply international cooperation to the problem of ensuring basic economic security. The United States proposes steps to safeguard against the economic shocks to which developing countries are particularly vulnerable; sharp declines in their export earnings from the cycle of world supply and demand, food shortages and natural disasters. Second, we must lay the foundations for accelerated growth. The United States proposes steps to improve developing countries' access to capital markets, to focus and

adapt new technology to specific development needs, and to reach consensus
on the conditions for foreign investment. Third, we must improve the basic
opportunities of the developing countries in the world trading system so they
can make their way by earnings instead of aid. Fourth, we must improve the
conditions of trade and investment in key commodities on which the economies of many developing countries are dependent, and we must set an
example in improving the production and availability of food. Fifth, let us
address the special needs of the poorest countries which are the most devas-
tated by current economic conditions, sharing the responsibility among old
and newly wealthy donors.[25]

The United States made a number of proposals in line with its own
thinking on a strategy for development:

- Creation of a new development security facility, within the International
  Monetary Fund, to stabilize overall export earnings. The facility would
  provide loans to help overcome the impact of export fluctuations up to $2.5
  billion and possibly more in a single year, with a potential of $10 billion
  in outstanding loans. The facility would replace the IMF's compensatory
  finance facility; it would not be available for industrial countries.
- Establishment of a consumer-producer forum for every key commodity.
- Rules on nontariff barriers should be adopted to provide special consideration for developing countries.
- Creation of an International Investment Trust to mobilize portfolio capital
  for investment in local enterprises. The International Finance Corporation
  (IFC) would manage it and perhaps provide seed capital, but most of its
  funds would come from government and private investors.
- The capital of the International Finance Corporation should be at least
  quadrupled to increase the flow of private resources to developing countries.
- The United States would be willing to participate in "a major new international effort" to expand raw material resources in developing countries, in
  which the World Bank and its affiliates, in concert with private sources,
  should play a fundamental role.
- The United States indicated its willingness to hold a major share in a world
  food reserve system. It proposed that to meet potential shortfalls in food
  grains, potential total world reserves must reach at least 30 million tons of
  wheat and rice, and consideration should also be given to the question
  whether a similar reserve was needed in coarse grain.
- The United States would contribute to and actively support the new UN
  Revolving Fund for Natural Resources, which would encourage the worldwide exploration and exploitation of minerals, and thus promote one of the
  most promising endeavors of economic development.

- Establishment of an International Energy Institute to assist developing countries in energy development.
- Establishment of an International Centre for Exchange of Technological Information for the sharing of research findings relevant to developing countries.
- Establishment of an International Industrialization Institute to accelerate industrialization in developing countries.

On transnational corporations, the United States reiterated its point of view that they had been powerful instruments of modernization, both in the industrial nations and in the developing countries. The United States was, however, prepared to meet the proper concerns of governments on whose territories transnational enterprises operated. "We affirm that enterprises must act in full accordance with the sovereignty of host Governments and take full account of their public policy. Countries are entitled to regulate the operations of transnational enterprises within their borders. But countries wishing the benefits of these enterprises should foster the conditions that attract and maintain their productive operation."[26]

Moynihan made a brief reference to the report of the Committee of 25 on structural reforms within the UN system and suggested that its recommendations be seriously considered. From the point of view of the United States,

> an improved United Nations organization must include rationalization of the United Nations' fragmented assistance programmes; strengthened leadership within the central Secretariat and the entire UN System for development and economic cooperation; streamlining of the Economic and Social Council; better consultative procedures to ensure effective agreement among members with a particular interest in a subject under consideration; and a mechanism for independent evaluation of the implementation of programmes.[27]

In conclusion, the U.S. representative said his government had not offered these proposals as an act of charity nor should they be received as if due (a reference to the demand from developing countries for automatic transfers). "Materially as well as morally, our destinies are intertwined. . . . We can say once more to the new nations: We have heard your voices. We embrace your hopes. We will join your efforts. We commit ourselves to our common success."[28]

The package presented by the United States through the Kissinger/ Moynihan speech was not in itself revolutionary. Some of the proposals, such as those relating to IMF and World Bank, had already been under discussion for some time, while others, formulated as working hypotheses, would clearly need detailed and complex negotiations. What was new in the speech was the

tone. The speech stressed the need for a dialogue; in this Kissinger was conso-
nant with Bouteflika. Though the political and economic implications of the
OPEC action were seen through two totally different perspectives by Kissinger
and Bouteflika, they both agreed on the interdependence theme and the need
for negotiations.

It is interesting to note that Kissinger's speech was drafted in such a way
that even where it seemed to indicate agreement with the proposals of the
Group of 77, it avoided using their language. Omission of any mention of
UNIDO or UNCTAD was also probably deliberate, as these two agencies are
clearly identified in the minds of U.S. policy makers with Third World demands. Reports indicate that U.S. Treasury Secretary Simon's association with
the proposals in the speech was obtained through long and serious negotiations
between him and Kissinger.[29]

The Kissinger/Moynihan speech was followed by that of Mariano Rumor, minister of foreign affairs of Italy, who spoke on behalf of the European
Economic Community.[30] Referring to the plight of the developing countries,
he stated that, while the industrialized countries were likely to show a small
surplus at the end of 1975, the deficit of the developing countries had not been
reduced. In fact, the deficit of the poorest countries would probably rise from
$28 billion in 1974 to $34 billion in 1975. Furthermore, there was no increase
in the gross national product of these countries in 1974.

"The time has come," he went on, "to recognize that monetary stability
and order, secure conditions for trade and international investments, a balanced distribution of resources—and thus political and social stability—are
interdependent objectives which cannot be achieved without a new, better
balanced, wiser and fairer international economic order."[31]

Speaking as the president of the Council of the European Economic
Community, he indicated that the aim pursued by the community and its
nine-member states at the Special Session, was the achievement of real progress
toward a more equitable pattern of international economic relations to
strengthen the position of the developing countries. The community attached
particular importance to the problems of the poorest developing countries and
felt that specific measures should be introduced to assist them.

With these objectives in view, he indicated the community was willing to
work on the following specific proposals:

- The community was prepared to promote and support international action
  to achieve for the benefit of all the developing countries which produced
  raw materials, improvement in the compensatory financial mechanisms of
  the International Monetary Fund.
- The community was willing to make constructive contributions to international discussions aimed at improving market access for primary and processed products from developing countries.

- On industrial cooperation and the transfer of technology, the aim should be to enhance the industrial development of Third World countries by improving the international division of labor. This could be achieved by creating expanding production capacity and by taking particular account of the employment problems facing both the developing and the industrialized countries.
- The community was prepared to participate, within the framework of UNCTAD, in any discussions on an international code of conduct on transfer of technologies, taking due account of the needs of the developing countries.
- On the volume of aid, the community was determined to achieve the target of 0.7 percent of GNP for public aid.
- The community favoured the ideas put forward by the World Bank for setting up a financing mechanism somewhere between the loans made by the bank and the credits granted by the International Development Association (IDA). It was also willing to contribute to the special IMF account to reduce the interest burden payable under the oil facility by the hardest hit countries.

The EEC thus went farther than the United States in accepting the official aid target and indicating its willingness to consider, if not to immediately accept, many of the proposals put forward by the Group of 77. Though the proposals relating to indexation were not directly alluded to, the EEC felt that the kind of mechanism that had been worked out through the Lomé Convention could be considered as one of the possibilities for stabilizing export earnings of developing countries. The EEC also supported proposals for expanding the capacity of the World Bank and IMF to deal with the monetary and economic problems of the developing countries. While, in the case of the World Bank, this would mean expanding its current capacity, in the case of IMF, this would mean to some extent converting it from a monetary institution into an aid-giving institution.

THE SOCIALIST CASE

The attitude of the socialist countries in Eastern Europe as expressed by the representative of the USSR, Yakov Malik, was consistent with the approach taken by them at earlier assembly sessions.[32] According to the USSR representative, the socialist countries were "natural allies" of developing countries.[33] He went on to say that "the present political situation in the world is particulary favourable for the solution of these problems. It is characterized by the continuing relaxation of tension, the diminishing danger of war and the affirmation of the principles of peaceful co-existence in international relations. To make political detente an irreversible process and to complement it by military detente, to take real steps towards limiting the nuclear arms race and averting a nuclear war, to reduce and subsequently end the arms race while working for general and complete disarmament is the order of the day."[34]

The Chinese statement emphasized "self-reliance" and was generally sympathetic to the objectives of the Group of 77.[35] Li Chiang, the minister for foreign trade of China did not comment on specific proposals; nor did the representative of the USSR.

NEGOTIATIONS

The statements in the plenary recognized poverty as a global concern and reflected the desire of both rich and poor nations to work together toward finding solutions to this many-sided, urgent, and complex problem. Though the positions of the two sides did not always converge, it was accepted that they were negotiating as equal partners. This was a significant advance over previous occasions, which had served as shouting matches between unequals. However, the gap between public positions of the industrialized countries and the developing countries had not been narrowed in any significant way. The task of narrowing this gap fell to the Ad Hoc Committee which was meeting downstairs.

Negotiations in the basement conference rooms primarily took place between the 27-member contact group of the Group of 77 and the 12-member contact group of Western European and Other countries (WEO). The socialist countries and China were not involved in these negotiations (1) because they publicly supported the position of the developing countries and (2) because they were not active participants in the financial and institutional arrangements that the developing countries wanted to be changed.

The Group of 77 had already presented its demands through its position paper circulated as part of the preparatory documents for the Special Session. The EEC position paper had also been made available in advance. The new element was the U.S. position as outlined in the Kissinger/Moynihan speech. In addition, the United States circulated another document called "an informal working paper submitted by the United States of America for negotiating purposes." This paper, which was circulated on the eighth day of the session, incorporated some of the terminology used by the Group of 77, and seemed to indicate U.S. acceptance of some of their radical proposals. The U.S. delegation, however, soon put an end to such speculation by insisting that the document was nothing more than a mechanism for "negotiating purposes." In any case, it was certainly instrumental in strengthening the impression that the United States was seriously interested in negotiations.

The major differences between the positions of industrialized countries and the developing countries related to questions of indexation, transfer of resources, role of transnational corporations, and debt rescheduling. Indexation was pointedly emphasized in the working paper of the Group of 77 in a way that the industrialized countries clearly found unacceptable. The program proposed in the working paper referred flatly to "indexation of the prices of commodity and raw material exports from developing countries to the prices of their imports from developed countries."[36]

The United States expressed its opposition to the idea, as did EEC members, including the foreign minister of the Federal Republic of Germany, Hans-Dietrich Genscher. However, the EEC working paper supported the idea of "remunerative prices" and referred to "ways of protecting purchasing power." The United States was in the beginning totally opposed to any direct or indirect mention of indexation, but eventually agreed to a study of direct and indirect indexation schemes, along with other options which would enable the international community to maintain the purchasing power of developing countries.

On the transfer of resources, the Group of 77 asked the industrialized countries to accept the 0.7 percent target for official assistance by 1978. The EEC working paper indicated the willingness of the EEC member countries to try to reach this target. The United States was not willing to make any such commitment, formal or informal. The final agreement incorporated in Resolution 3362 (S-VII) asked developed countries to "confirm their continued commitment in respect of the targets relating to the transfer of resources, in particular the official development assistance target of 0.7 percent of GNP, as agreed in the International Development Strategy for the Second United Nations Decade, and adopt as their common aim an effective increase in official development assistance, with a view to achieving these targets by the end of the Decade." The United States still maintained its reservation, and in their statements at the conclusion of the Seventh Special Session, both Ambassadors Myerson and Moynihan indicated that though the United States was willing to work toward an increase in official aid, it did not want to be tied down to a target.

The position paper of the Group of 77 referred to automatic mechanisms for the transfer of real resources, which should be adopted and implemented through agreements on the establishment of a link between the Special Drawing Rights (SDR)* and the development assistance. A number of industrial-

---

*The SDR, which is used by IMF as a unit of account, was at its inception linked to the gold content of the dollar through the stipulation that one SDR shall be equivalent to 0.888671 gram of fine gold. Following the suspension of the convertibility of the dollar into gold, the method of valuation of the SDR was changed in 1974. The value of one SDR now consists of 40 U.S. cents, 38 German pfennig, 4.5 British pence, 44 French centimes, 26 Japanese yen, and smaller amounts of some other currencies. The value calculated at the current rate of exchange is published daily by IMF.

ized countries had reservations on this clause. The final resolution says, "the establishment of a link between the special drawing rights and development assistance should form part of the consideration by the IMF of the creation of new special drawing rights as and when they are established, according to the needs of international liquidity."

Any direct reference to debt rescheduling was avoided because of U.S. opposition, and the resolution recommended that UNCTAD IV consider the possibility of convening, as soon as possible, a conference of major donor, creditor, and debtor countries to devise ways and means to mitigate the debt burden, taking into account the development needs of developing countries, with special attention to the plight of the most seriously affected countries.

On the role of transnational corporations, agreement was difficult to achieve. The final resolution does not say much on this subject, thus leaving it open for further discussions.

The people who played the most visible role in the discussions and negotiations in and around the Ad Hoc Committee were Jan Pronk, the Dutch minister for development cooperation, Manuel Perez Guerrero, the Venezuelan minister of state for economic planning, and Ambassador Iqbal Akhund, president of the Economic and Social Council. Toward the very end, Thomas Enders, a top Kissinger aide, joined the U.S. side to participate in the hard bargaining. He was brought in, probably because he was most familiar with the detailed and difficult negotiating process that had taken place in Washington within the U.S. government to develop the U.S. position. The patience and ingenuity required to find a text acceptable to all taxed the skills of these and other negotiators a great deal; but finally a draft was worked out that was generally acceptable to the major interested governments, including the United States.

Members of the UN or United Nations Development Programme (UNDP) Secretariats did not play a significant role in these informal discussions and negotiations. A task force within the UN Secretariat, working under the leadership of Bradford Morse, then under secretary general for political and General Assembly affairs, had made sure that the assembly was well-prepared and well-managed. But early in 1975 it seems to have been agreed that neither the secretary general nor his staff would take positions on substantive issues in the political debate preparatory to and during the Special Session. The secretary general made an opening and a closing speech, but in between did not participate in any of the informal discussions. The UNDP leadership also kept itself aloof from these discussions. The only senior UN system official who actively participated in the session was Gamani Corea, secretary general of UNCTAD; he had the advantage and the disadvantage of being closely identified with the position of the Group of 77.

The resolution adopted by the Special Session draws on facts and figures provided in various UN documents, but in its orientation and approach it is very much the end product of a process of negotiations which took as its basis the demands from the Group of 77 and revised them to make them acceptable to most of the industrialized countries. On those issues where agreement was clearly impossible, the resolution provides for continuing discussions.

One of the reasons for the success of the negotiations at the Special Session was that they avoided ideological considerations and concentrated on specific issues. This was as true of the developed countries as of the developing. The public debate produced some saber rattling, but the informal discussions were not vitiated by empty threats and meaningless slogans.

The OPEC countries, including the Arabs, proved flexible and pragmatic; and they received unequivocal support from other developing countries. As it became evident that the links between the OPEC countries and other developing countries could not be broken, the negotiators on the other side took this as a fact of life and focused on the task of bringing the negotiations to a successful conclusion.

On the side of the industrialized countries, the Americans were the main negotiators. They were patient and open to new suggestions on how to break deadlocks. Among the Europeans, the Dutch and the Scandinavians were ahead of the others, and often managed to persuade other Western Europeans to come along.

FINAL RESOLUTION

The resolution, as has already been mentioned, consists of seven parts (see Appendix B). Six of these relate to the six topics on the agenda; an extra section deals with cooperation among developing countries.

On international trade, the resolution calls for concerted efforts in favor of the developing countries—"toward expanding and diversifying their trade, improving and diversifying their productive capacity, improving their productivity, and increasing their export earnings." It also calls for concerted action toward accelerating the growth and diversification of the export trade of developing countries in manufactures and semimanufactures, and in processed and semiprocessed products in order to increase their share in world industrial output, and world trade within the framework of an expanding world economy.

These general aims were easily agreed to by all the parties, but more specific issues were referred to the Fourth Session of UNCTAD or to the secretariat of UNCTAD. UNCTAD IV was asked to reach decisions on the improvement of market structures in the field of raw materials and commodities of export interest to the developing countries, with particular reference to the following:

a. Appropriate international stocking and other forms of market arrangements for securing stable, remunerative, and equitable prices for commodities of export interest to developing countries and promoting equilibrium between supply and demand, including, where possible, long-term multilateral commitments;

b. Adequate international financing facilities for such stocking and market arrangements;

c. Where possible, promotion of long-term and medium-term contracts;

d. Substantial improvement of facilities for compensatory financing of export revenue fluctuations through the widening and enlarging of the existing facilities. Note has been taken of the various proposals regarding a comprehensive scheme for the stabilization of export earnings of developing countries and for a Development Security Facility as well as specific measures for the benefit of the developing countries most in need;

e. Promotion of processing of raw materials in producing developing countries and expansion and diversification of their exports, particularly to developed countries;

f. Effective opportunities to improve the share of developing countries in transport, marketing, and distribution of their primary commodities and to encourage measures of world significance for the evolution of the infrastructure and secondary capacity of developing countries from the production of primary commodities to processing, transport and marketing, and to the production of finished manufactured goods, their transport, distribution and exchange, including advanced financial and exchange institutions for the remunerative management of trade transactions.

The UNCTAD Secretariat was asked to study: (a) the impact of an integrated program on the imports of developing countries, (b) direct and indirect indexation schemes and other options, and (c) the proportion between prices of raw materials and commodities exported by developing countries and the final consumer price, particularly in developed countries.

As for the developed countries, they were asked to reduce or remove, where possible or appropriate, nontariff barriers affecting developing countries' exports. The resolution also asks that the Generalized Scheme of Preferences (GSP) should not terminate at the end of the period of ten years as originally envisaged, but should be continued and continually improved. "Countervailing duties should be applied only in conformity with internationally agreed obligations"; and "restrictive business practices adversely affecting international trade, particularly that of developing countries, should be eliminated." The section on international trade also refers to the need for emergency measures, and to the desirability of further expansion of trade between the socialist countries of Eastern Europe and the developing countries.

On the transfer of resources, the resolution states that "concessional financial resources to developing countries need to be increased substantially" and that "financial assistance should, as a general rule, be untied." The resolution reconfirmed the official development assistance target of 0.7 percent of GNP and asked the developed countries to increase assistance with a view to reaching this target by the end of the decade. With an eye on the United States, the resolution says that "developed countries which have not yet made a commitment in respect of their targets (should) undertake to make their best efforts to reach these targets in the remaining part of this Decade."

The establishment of a link between the special drawing rights and development assistance was another demand of the Group of 77 and is included in the resolution. As noted earlier, the United States and several other industrialized countries were not willing to accept such a link, and in his final statement in the Ad Hoc Committee, Ambassador Myerson made this quite clear.

Another part of the resolution says that "developed countries and international organizations should enhance the real value and volume of assistance to developing countries and ensure that the developing countries obtain the largest possible share in the procurement of equipment, consultants, and consultancy services." There has been increasing criticism of the amounts spent on international experts or on procurement of costly equipment from specified countries, and this section reflects this dissatisfaction.

Some of the more specific proposals included in the section on transfer of real resources are listed below:

Agreement should be reached at an early date on the establishment of a trust fund to be financed partly through the IMF gold sales and partly through voluntary contributions and to be governed by an appropriate body, for the benefit of developing countries.

Substantial increases in the capital of the World Bank group and in particular the resources of the IDA should be made.

The resources of the development institutions of the United Nations System, in particular the UNDP, should also be increased. The funds at the disposal of the regional development banks should be augmented. The resolution makes the point that these increases should be without prejudice to bilateral development assistance flows.

Consideration should be given to the idea of establishing an international investment trust and to the expansion of the IFC capital.

The compensatory financing facility now available through the IMF should be expanded and liberalized.

The IMF should expedite its study of the possibility of an amendment of the Articles of Agreement, to be presented to the Interim Committee, if possible at its next meeting, that would permit the fund to provide assistance directly to international buffer stocks of primary products.

An important point on future monetary arrangements that the resolution mentions is that the role of national reserve currencies should be reduced and the special drawing rights should become the central reserve asset of the international monetary system in order to provide for greater international control over the creation and equitable distribution of liquidity, and in order to limit potential losses as a consequence of exchange rate fluctuations. Furthermore, "arrangements for gold should be consistent with the agreed objective of reducing the role of gold in the system and with equitable distribution of new international liquidity."

On decision making, the resolution asks that the process be fair and responsive to change. "The participation of developing countries in the decision-making process in the competent organs of international finance and development institutions should be adequately increased and made more effective without adversely affecting the broad geographic representation of developing countries, and in accordance with the existing and evolving rules."

On science and technology, the resolution calls for a significant expansion of the assistance from developed countries to developing countries in support of their science and technology programs. The specific proposals included in this section are consideration of the possibility of establishing an international center for the exchange of technological information, a preliminary study on the possibility of establishing within the UN system an international energy institute, and a United Nations Conference on Science and Technology for Development in 1978 and 1979. A major role for the United Nations system is foreseen in most of the ideas and proposals listed under this section.

On industrialization, the resolution endorses the Lima Declaration and Plan of Action on Industrial Development Cooperation. Redeployment of some industries from developed countries to developing countries is encouraged, as is a system of consultations between developed and developing countries, and among developing countries themselves, to facilitate industrialization.

Most of the section focuses on activities to be undertaken by UNIDO. It endorses the proposal to convert UNIDO into a specialized agency of the United Nations. The assembly decided to establish an intergovernmental committee of all member governments to draw up a constitution for UNIDO as a specialized agency for submission to a plenipotentiary conference in the last quarter of 1976.

On food and agriculture, the resolution affirms the premise that "the solution to world food problems lies primarily in increasing rapidly food production in the developing countries." To this end, the resolution calls for a substantial increase in the volume of assistance to developing countries for agriculture and food production, access to the markets of developed countries for food and agricultural products of developing countries, stable supply of fertilizers and other production inputs to developing countries at reasonable prices, and expansion of the work of existing international agricultural research centers.

The resolution calls for pledges of voluntary contributions to the proposed IFAD so that it could come into being at the end of 1975, with initial resources of SDR 1,000 million (approximately $1.25 billion).

The resolution emphasizes the importance of food aid as a transitional measure and calls upon all countries to accept both the principle of a minimum food aid target and the concept of forward planning of food aid. The target for the 1975–76 season should be 10 million tons of food grains, a figure mentioned during the World Food Conference in 1974. The resolution also asks those countries in a position to do so to provide food grains and financial assistance on most favorable terms to the most seriously affected countries, the proviso being that food aid should be provided in such a way as to avoid causing undue fluctuations in market prices or the disruption of commercial markets for food exports from developing countries.

The resolution endorses the concept of an international undertaking on world food security and, pending the establishment of a world food grain reserve, asks for earmarking of stocks and/or funds to be placed at the disposal of the World Food Programme (WFP), as an emergency measure to strengthen the capacity of the program to deal with crisis situations in developing countries. The target in the first instance is 500,000 tons in emergency reserve.

The section on cooperation among developing countries emphasizes the importance of mutual cooperation among developing countries at subregional, regional, and interregional levels, and asks the developed countries and the entire United Nations system to provide, as and when requested, suitable support and assistance for the promotion of such cooperation.

The last section on the "restructuring of the economic and social sectors of the UN System" calls for the establishment of an Ad Hoc Committee to consider all the aspects of restructuring. This committee, which was established by the 1975 Assembly as a committee of the whole (open to the participation of all states), met several times during 1975 and 1976 and, as requested, submitted its final report to the 1976 Assembly Session. Its work is dealt with in Chapter 7.

Though the resolution was adopted without a vote, several countries were not able to accept all the points mentioned in the resolution. Japan and some members of the European Community expressed their inability to reach the aid target of 0.7 percent of GNP. The United States also could not accept the target, though it supported the objective. The United States also expressed its reservations on indexation, SDR/aid link, and the UNIDO system of consultations. U.S. Ambassador Myerson, in his statement in the Ad Hoc Committee on September 16, 1975,[37] mentioned several other points where the U.S. opinion differed from those expressed in the resolution. The United States did not fully agree with the paragraph dealing with decision-making in international financial institutions: "We support an evolving role for developing nations. We believe, however, that participation and decision-making must be equitable for all members and take due account of relative economic positions and contributions of resources to the institutions as well as the need for efficient operational decision-making." On redeployment of industries, Myerson said: "This should be a matter of evolution of economies rather than a question of international policy or negotiation."

Despite these reservations, the United States supported the resolution and this was eloquently expressed in the final statement of Ambassador Moynihan in the plenary.

Secretary General Waldheim emphasized the significance of the agreements reached at the Special Session by stating:

> The problems connected with the new international economic order are now being tackled by all governments at the highest level of political responsibility. Indeed, the world's attention is today more than it has ever been focused on the problems of poverty and development which dictate a new course in international relationships. They are finally reaching the head of the agenda of the international community.[38]

President of the General Assembly Bouteflika also expressed his satisfaction with the resolution. In his speech at the closing of the assembly's 29th session (which followed the closing of the Special Session), he made the point that the Third World countries do not form a homogenous or regimented bloc, and their solidarity holds together "because they are experiencing the same problems, confronting the same difficulties and pursuing the same goals."[39]

Jan Pronk, who was the chairman of the Ad Hoc Committee talked at a press conference of a "commitment to commit" efforts toward change. For him, the Special Session was "quite an important happening," and as a result, future negotiations included those at UNCTAD IV would be "different" from what they would otherwise have been.[40]

Because of the uncertainty which had prevailed at the beginning of the Seventh Special Session as to the results of the session, there was a natural tendency on the part of all concerned to feel relieved, even jubilant, about the spirit of consensus which had developed. The Resolution on Development and International Economic Cooperation was widely publicized as a major breakthrough in international economic negotiations.

However, there was also the realization, particularly among the representatives of the developing countries, that what lay ahead was a process of continuing negotiations and hard bargaining. Ambassador Iqbal Akhund em-

phasized, in a television program recorded by the UN soon after the Seventh
Special Session, that much more needed to be done.

> And to do that, we have, in the rest of the year, and in the coming year, a
> number of meetings and conferences of one kind or another scheduled. . . .
> So we have the forums at which agreements on world principles, and in some
> cases more detailed agreements, can be worked out and translated into
> practical decisions.[41]

A close reading of the text of the resolution, along with the position papers
or working documents of the Group of 77, EEC, and the United States, shows
that most of the policy statements advocated by the Group of 77 were incorporated in the resolution. The resolution also included suggestions for the
strengthening and expansion of several of the existing international monetary
and financial institutions, and for the establishment of several new institutions
that were needed. On changes in international monetary arrangements, the
resolution stressed a number of proposals which have since come to pass.
However, on the thornier questions of commodity trade and aid in general, the
resolution basically reiterated the need for further negotiations.

The resolution did not touch upon several questions of major concern to
the international community. Environmental problems, which led to the convening of the UN Conference on Human Environment (Stockholm, June 1972)
under the energetic and imaginative leadership of Maurice Strong, and to the
establishment of the United Nations Environment Programme (UNEP) toward the end of the same year, were not mentioned. Population, the theme of
the World Population Conference (Bucharest, August 1974), was mentioned
in a few speeches, but the resolution does not refer to the World Plan of Action
adopted at the Bucharest Conference or to the continuing UN program in the
field. Women's integration in development, the theme of the International
Women's Year Conference (Mexico, June 1975), was also totally ignored.

There may have been a feeling that since these questions were thoroughly
debated and discussed at previous UN conferences, there was no need to
consider them again. Many of the Third World delegates also felt that the focus
of the Seventh Special Session was on transfer of resources from the rich to
the poor countries, and nothing should be allowed to divert them from a
dialogue on this subject with the representatives of the industrialized countries.

There are other, perhaps even more valid, explanations. Environment is
still considered by many in the Third World as primarily a Western concern,
and there are even those who talk about "a little pollution" being good for their
development, since this presupposes industrial growth. Environmental concerns including pollution control, conservation, and proper utilization of resources, cannot however be regarded as the exclusive concerns of the rich
world. The Stockholm Conference emphasized the fact that environmental

problems do not know or respect any national boundaries, and their solutions must be found in a worldwide context.

Population, despite the Bucharest Conference, is still regarded in many circles as a controversial or embarrassing topic. But how can a program of action on a new international economic order avoid dealing with the problem of population growth? The pressure of the growing numbers of people on the world's resources is one of the major factors which brought governmental representatives together at the Seventh Special Session; and whether it is planning for increased agricultural production or for industrial growth, population factors will have to be taken fully into account.

The question of women's participation in the development process is sometimes brushed aside on the ground that a new economic order, when it comes about, will automatically take care of the needs and rights of women, along with the rest of the people. But as the International Women's Year campaign led by Mrs. Helvi Sipila so convincingly demonstrated, special attention needs to be paid to the problem of improving the status of women; and consistent and vigorous national and international action is needed to ensure that women are given complete equality, and have the opportunity to play a full role in economic and social development. How can we indeed talk about a new economic order without taking into account the role of one-half of humanity?

SUMMING UP

The consensus formula, which was used to hammer out the text of the resolution, may serve as a precedent for future negotiations on economic issues. Indeed, at the Paris talks in December 1975, and the meeting of the 20-member Interim Committee of the IMF in Kingston in January 1976, decisions were arrived at in the same way—tortuous, difficult negotiations leading to compromise and consensus.

In summary, the resolution was significant in three ways:

1. it formalized the desire for a radical change in the international economic order,
2. it specified the areas where continuing negotiations were needed, and
3. presented a framework in which institutional changes and innovations could take place.

The resolution would not bring about a new economic order by itself. Nor would it go down in the history of the United Nations as one that specified profound changes. It was, however, an indicator of the major shifts in the political and economic alignments that had taken place in the world since

World War II. In this sense, it also serves as a precursor of a new era in political and economic relations, based on interdependence.

The Seventh Special Session started a chain of actions and events which, in due course, could bring about profound changes in the international economic and financial structures, and trade and aid patterns. It is, however, clear that these changes will not come about easily, because those who possess money and power today are not going to give these up voluntarily and easily, and those who do not will have to live through many frustrations and disappointments, and continue to maintain their cohesion before they accomplish some of their objectives.

The Special Session provided a framework for intergovernmental negotiations as do all the other major conferences dealing with economic, financial, trade, and development issues; but if fundamental changes are to come about, they can not be brought about by governmental action alone. In the industrialized countries, the changes and adjustments that will be needed in the economies cannot be initiated unless citizens and organized sectors such as media, trade unions, and employer groups accept them. This in turn will require a wide-ranging discussion of issues relating to international division of labor, trade, production, employment, and so forth. Economic changes that come about will probably cause social dislocation and upheaval. For example, workers in those industries that no longer remain profitable because of competition from developing countries will have to be retrained and relocated; this is not going to be easy. Farmers who are accustomed to receiving high government subsidies may have to live with lower subsidies in the future; this again will not be easy to sell. Consumption of energy, as well as of goods and services, will have to be cut down, and this will militate against well-established habits and customs; but all of this will need to be accomplished if a new economic order is to acquire real substance.

The Third World countries themselves will have to bring about major economic and social changes within their own boundaries. The discussion on a new international economic order basically is about transfer of goods, services, and technology from one group of countries to another. How the benefits of this transfer are going to be made available to the masses in the Third World is a question that was not touched on at all, in any meaningful way, in the Seventh Special Session. Though the concept of quantitative development is giving way to that of qualitative development, the leaders of Third World societies need to undertake practical steps to ensure that the minimum needs of their peoples are met in the context of their own economic, social, and cultural needs, and that overall development of their societies is linked to projects that emphasize self-reliance, even though international aid and assistance may play some role in spurring some sectors of their economies.

Collectively, the Third World countries need to maintain their cohesion and to strengthen their bargaining power. They also need to promote and strengthen practical cooperation among themselves. A major step in this direction was taken at the Manila Conference of the Group of 77 in February 1976, when a resolution was adopted on "economic cooperation among developing countries." As a follow-up to Manila, an Intergovernmental Working Group is to work out further details of the program suggested in Manila.

Further research, education, and public information activities are needed which will seek to focus attention on new needs and requirements, as well as the new policies needed. A reorganized UN system could be of great help in these areas, as in the area of promoting projects with an emphasis on collective self-reliance.

The following analysis of the developments since the Seventh Special Session attempts to show how these objectives and possibilities are being developed in various sectors.

NOTES

1. *U.S. Mission to the United Nations,* Press release September 16, 1975; USUN-94(75), UN Doc. A/PV.2349, pp. 27–30.

2. "Development and Cooperation: The Seventh Special Session," text of a television commentary produced by UNTV and CESI, p. 11.

3. UN Doc. E/AC.62/L.5 and Corr.1, August 28, 1975.

4. The verbatim reports of the Seventh Special Session are contained in UN Docs. A/PV.2326-2349, September 1–16, 1975.

5. For the text of Bouteflika's speech, see UN Doc. A/PV.2326, September 1, 1975, pp. 11–32.

6. Ibid., pp. 13–15.

7. Ibid., p. 16.

8. Ibid., p. 18–20.

9. Ibid., p. 21.

10. For the text of Waldheim's speech, see UN Doc. A/PV.2326, September 1, 1975, pp. 33–45.

11. Ibid., pp. 38–40.

12. For the text of Azeredo Da Silveira's speech, see UN Doc. A/PV.2327, September 1, 1975, pp. 2–16.

13. Ibid., p. 6.

14. Ibid., p. 6.

15. Ibid., p. 16.

16. For the text of Guerrero's speech, see UN Doc. A/PV.2327, September 1, 1975, pp. 91–105.

17. Ibid., p. 101.

18. For the text of Amouzegar's speech, see UN Doc. A/PV.2328, September 2, 1975, pp. 2–15.

19. Ibid., p. 6.

20. For the text of Chavan's speech, see UN Doc. A/PV.2328, September 2, 1975, pp. 51–67.

21. Ibid., p. 53.

22. Ibid., p. 56.

23. For the text of Moynihan's speech, see UN Doc. A/PV.2327, September 1, 1975, pp. 16–65.

24. Ibid., p. 22.

25. Ibid., p. 23.

26. Ibid., p. 38.

27. Ibid., p. 61.

28. Ibid., p. 63–65.

29. *The Inter Dependent,* October 1975, p. 1.

30. For the text of Rumor's speech, see UN Doc. A/PV.2327, September 1, 1975, pp. 66–90.

31. Ibid., p. 71.

32. For the text of Malik's speech see UN Doc. A/PV.2330, September 3, 1975, pp. 22–45.

33. Ibid., p. 23–25.

34. Ibid., p. 26.

35. For the text of Li Chiang's speech see UN Doc. A/PV.2329, September 16, 1975, pp. 16–40.

36. UN Doc. E/5749, August 29, 1975, p. 12.

37. *U.S. Mission to the UN,* Press release USUN-93(75), September 16, 1975.

38. UN Doc. A/PV.2349, September 16, 1975. p. 42.

39. UN Press release GA/5306, September 16, 1975.

40. See United Nations, General Assembly, Seventh Special Session, *Round-up and Resolution* (New York, 1975), p. 15.

41. "Development and Cooperation: The Seventh Special Session," op. cit., p. 11.

Three separate but interrelated developments stand out as we look at the continuing international effort to give substance to the Resolution on Development and International Economic Cooperation adopted by the Seventh Special Session (see Appendix B): First, a series of meetings between September 1975 and January 1976 which sought to bring about changes in the structure and operations of the World Bank Group and the International Monetary Fund. Second, the Paris Conference on International Economic Cooperation which took place in December 1975 and established four commissions to work on energy, raw materials, finance, and development. Third, UNCTAD IV, in Nairobi, and preparatory to it a major conference of the developing countries which was held in Manila in February 1976. Many of the participants at all these meetings were the same. Several of the finance ministers and foreign ministers who attended the IMF meetings also attended the Paris conference, were at Manila, and also at Nairobi. However, the setting has been somewhat different in each case. In the World Bank and IMF, the industrialized countries control the institutional structures and hold the majority of the votes; and the representatives of the developing countries who participate in their meetings find that changes can be brought about only gradually. The Paris conference served as a new experiment in the process of international bargaining on economic and financial issues, and consensus arrived at through tortuous negotiations was the rule. UNCTAD has, on the other hand, been the forum where the Group of 77 holds sway. The industrialized countries at past UNCTAD meetings have had to react to demands for sweeping changes in the international trade and economic structures brought forward by the Group of 77, and their strategy has been generally to offer stubborn resistance. This time, however, efforts were made to ensure prior consultations and discussions, in order to bring about progress on at least some issues at UNCTAD IV.

THE WORLD BANK AND THE IMF

While the Seventh Special Session was meeting in New York, the governors of the World Bank and the International Monetary Fund gathered in Washington for their annual meetings (September 1–5, 1975). Many of the issues on their agenda were the same as those raised at the Special Session; and the decisions taken by them relate closely to some of the concerns and suggestions expressed through the assembly resolution on Development and International Economic Cooperation[1] (see Appendix B).

The changes and reforms that are reflected in these decisions form part of a process that seeks to transform the structures and operations of the monetary and financial institutions which were originally established by the Western industrialized countries to fulfill the needs of postwar economic reconstruction and to regulate exchange and monetary requirements from their perspective.

The institutions that were created as a result of the Bretton Woods Conference in 1944 were concerned with two requirements prescribed by the United States and other industrialized countries. The immediate requirement was postwar reconstruction, and the bank established through the conference decisions was aptly given the name of International Bank for Reconstruction and Development (popularly known as the World Bank). The long-term need was to establish a stable monetary system for regulated and orderly international trade. The 1944 agreement made the dollar—the strongest currency at that time—convertible into gold at $35 an ounce. All other countries were required to choose an exchange rate for their currencies in relation to both the dollar and gold. The exchange system was thus pegged to the convertible dollar.

After its initial involvement in the reconstruction of Europe, the role of the World Bank changed and expanded in the sixties, and as the demands from developing countries for development capital and aid grew, the World Bank responded by expanding its lending operations and by establishing other institutions which could relate more directly to needs and requirements of the developing countries. Particularly since Robert McNamara became the president of the bank, it has become more seriously involved in development activities.

The bank borrows its funds in the international capital markets and relends them to developing countries for financing development projects. The interest rates and repayment terms cover the cost of its administration, as well as its obligations on the funds raised. The bank thus operates on a commercial basis and its interest rates are generally high. Two other subsidiaries of the bank, the IDA and the IFC, fulfill functions more closely related to developing countries' requirements.

The IDA raises money from governments and relends it to the poorer developing countries (such as India, Bangladesh, and smaller Asian and African countries) with a small service charge and at no interest. It replenishes its funds on an average every three years, by asking governments for funds for its soft-loan operations. The IFC encourages private investments in developing countries and has the authority to take equity positions in private enterprises in developing countries.

At the September meetings, expansion plans were announced for each of the World Bank group institutions. The bank plans to increase its capital by $8.3 billion to $39.2 billion, a good part of the new capital to come from OPEC countries. IDA would launch its fifth "replenishment." Last time this operation yielded $3.5 billion. The aim this time is to get more to make up for inflation, and to meet additional needs of developing countries. IFC also plans to enlarge its capital base from $480 million to $587 million. All of these developments relate to the proposals mentioned by the United States and the EEC during the Seventh Special Session and incorporated in the final resolution.

One of the more imaginative ventures of the World Bank group was the establishment of a Third Window between the World Bank and IDA. This operation will provide loans at a subsidized interest rate to those countries that are not eligible for IDA loans and that cannot meet the bank's harder terms. The operation is financed through a special fund put up by some ten countries which promised to subscribe $125 million in the first instance. The operation will lend around $1 billion, at a concessionary rate of about 4.5 percent.

The World Bank has thus become closely involved in providing development capital through all its institutions. The IMF is, on the other hand, basically a mechanism for regulating exchange rates. In the earlier chapter, we mentioned several proposals made at the Special Session, which would partially convert IMF into an aid-giving institution. These were agreed upon at the IMF annual meeting in September 1975.

On the future of gold, it was agreed that it would play a reduced role in the international monetary system. The official price of gold, which had risen from $35 an ounce to $42.50, was abandoned, as it bore no relationship with the market price—almost four times the official price. The fund also decided to divest itself of one-third of its total gold holdings. One-sixth of those gold holdings will be distributed back to its members in proportion to their quotas; the other one-sixth will be sold in the market and the funds obtained through such sale placed in a trust fund, from which special loans can be made to the most seriously affected countries (MSAs). The central banks are now free to buy and sell gold in the open market; but the governors of the ten largest central banks agreed among themselves not to add to the total stock with the central banks over the next two years.

Of more immediate interest to the developing countries was the decision of the IMF to raise its total resources from $38 billion to $50 billion through an increase in its quotas for member countries. It also decided to continue the "special oil facility" that was established in 1974 to help countries facing difficulties because of the rise in the fuel import costs. The facility provided $3 billion in 1974 at 7 percent and another $6 billion in 1975 at 7.5 percent. The fund also agreed to establish a subsidiary scheme attached to the oil facility so that the poorer countries could get oil facility loans at around 2.5 percent interest rate instead of the more general 7.5 percent interest rate.

The compensatory financing facility of IMF was not reviewed in September; but soon afterward the IMF executive directors approved a major expansion of the facility. The facility was established in 1963 to support countries that suffered from fluctuations in commodity prices caused by circumstances largely beyond their control (for example, a fall in world prices, foreign competition, recession, and so forth). Under this scheme, an eligible member was allowed to draw foreign currencies up to 50 percent of its quota, but drawings could not exceed 25 percent of its quota in any 12-month period, except in case of major emergencies. These rules were liberalized at the end of 1975 to permit drawings up to 75 percent of a member's quota, provided that total drawings would not exceed 50 percent of the quota in any 12-month period.[2] The net result of these decisions has been, first, to increase the resources available through IMF for improving the general liquidity position of all countries, and second, to provide special facilities for developing countries.

No agreements were reached in September 1975 on the linking of SDRs with development assistance. In the view of the industrialized countries, the IMF's establishment of a trust fund out of the gold sale operation is to serve, at least temporarily, the purpose the developing countries have in mind, in asking for such a link.

Another decision taken in Washington responds to the demand from the developing countries that the process of decision making be fair and responsive to change. The voting power of OPEC countries in IMF was doubled from 5 percent to 10 percent. In practice, this would mean that the developing countries (including OPEC members) will now hold 32.5 percent of the total votes. On the other hand, American interests were safeguarded by a decision that gave the United States a veto power over all major decisions by prescribing that such decisions could not be reached except through an 85-percent majority. The voting quotas in the bank are also to change gradually, in favor of the developing countries.

Several of the agreements, which were arrived at during the September meeting in Washington, came up for review and further action at two subsequent meetings, prior to the end of 1975. The Western Finance Ministers meeting in Paris, on December 19, 1975, agreed to the sale of one-sixth of the IMF gold stock or 25 million ounces, beginning in February 1976, for the benefit of poor nations. This group, known as the Group of 10, includes the United States, France, the German Federal Republic, the United Kingdom, Italy, the Netherlands, Belgium, Sweden, Canada, and Japan.

The Interim Committee of IMF, which includes representatives of both developed and developing countries, and is known as the Group of 20, met in Kingston, Jamaica, in January 1976.[3] The committee agreed on a formal revision of the charter of the fund, authorizing countries to float their currencies according to market supply and demand. This is a recognition of the reality that has prevailed since the beginning of 1973. The U.S. dollar and several of the European currencies have been floating since then in technical violation of the IMF charter. The Kingston agreement legitimizes this situation. For several months the agreement had been held up because of differences between the United States and France; but the French finally agreed at the Paris meeting of the Western Finance Ministers to recognize floating exchange rates, and there was no controversy in Kingston on this question.

There were two other areas where agreements were reached after intensive discussions in Kingston. The first related to the liberalization of the IMF lending terms. Under the IMF charter, member countries with balance-of-payments difficulties are allowed to obtain credit from the fund in four segments (or tranches), each equal to 25 percent of a member's quota. Withdrawal of the first segment is relatively easy, and conditions become tougher as a country proceeds to withdraw further segments or tranches. The Kingston agreement provides for an increase of 45 percent in each of the four tranches. This should primarily benefit the non-oil-producing developing countries. According to the managing director of IMF, H. Johannes Witteveen, the agreement is expected to increase their potential borrowing power by about $3.5 billion.[4] Members will have access to this facility until the agreement to raise the members' quotas by one-third takes effect, within 18 to 24 months.

The second agreement relates to the currencies IMF can use in providing loans. The United States had argued that IMF should be able to use the currencies of oil-producing countries, with huge balance-of-payments surpluses. It was finally agreed that the currencies of the oil-producing countries would be made available for loans through IMF, "within six months." This problem will not arise once the IMF articles are amended, because under the revised articles, all members will be obligated to provide their currencies for IMF lending purposes.

The reforms agreed upon in Kingston were praised by many of the industrialized countries. U.S. Secretary of the Treasury William E. Simon told reporters that he was very well satisfied; "we achieved the ultimate monetary reform that we all came to accomplish." The French finance minister, Jean-Pierre Fourcade, welcomed the agreement as "the end of a debate lasting three years." The Belgian finance minister, Willy Declerq, who chaired the meeting in Kingston, described it as "the end of a very long road to monetary reform that was achieved, thanks to the political will to succeed."[5]

In expressing their satisfaction in such an effusive manner, these finance ministers were also indicating their resistance to further proposals for reform in the IMF System. Indeed, William Simon said quite openly that he did not foresee any further major initiatives toward reforming the international monetary system in the near future.[6]

As for the developing countries, their reaction was somewhat muted. They welcomed the agreement to sell one-sixth of the IMF gold stock, and the agreement to enable member countries with balance-of-payments difficulties to obtain credit from the fund on more liberal terms. As the special "oil facility" expired in February 1976, easier credit from IMF would help serve a vital need of many non-oil-producing countries.

Most of the developing countries did not have a say in the agreement concerning the floating of exchange rates. At the September meeting of IMF, they had spoken along with the French in favour of stable but adjustable parities. But the French changed their position by the beginning of 1976; and the developing country representatives were not willing to fight a battle on their own.

PARIS CONFERENCE

While the World Bank- and IMF-related meetings in Washington, Paris, and Kingston represented a set of efforts aimed at reforming the international monetary system and providing larger and easier credit for the developing countries, the Paris conference and the subsequent negotiations provide a forum for continuing negotiations between industrialized and developing countries on economic and financial issues of crucial importance over the next few years. The United States—as mentioned earlier—wanted to restrict the Paris talks to a discussion of the energy problem. This was, however, shot down by the developing countries very early on, and the United States and other industrialized countries agreed to expand the agenda to include raw materials, development, and financing. The Paris conference, which was called the Conference on International Economic Cooperation, took place from December 16 to 18, 1975. It was attended by 27 countries—8 representing the Western industrialized countries and 19 representing the developing countries, 8 of which were members of OPEC.

Soon after its inauguration by French President Valery Giscard d'Estaing, the conference became embroiled in a procedural question, which illustrated many of the difficulties that negotiators on the two sides faced in the months ahead. The point of contention was the mandate of the four commissions on energy, raw materials, finance, and development. While the industrialized countries wanted each commission to work out its own agenda, the developing countries wanted the conference itself to reach agreement on a specific mandate for the commissions. The two cochairmen of the conference—Allan

MacEachen (Canada) and Manuel Perez Guerrero (Venezuela)—negotiated with their respective groups and between themselves, and finally came up with a compromise. The conference agreed to the formation of a coordinating committee consisting of the cochairmen of the conference and of its commissions, ten in all.[7] The committee was asked to meet on January 26, 1976, to work out the mandate for the four commissions, and the commissions were to start work on February 11. If the committee could not reach any agreement on the mandate of the commissions, the negotiations would go ahead without specific guidelines.

The conference heard a number of presentations, but did not have the time or the opportunity to discuss any proposals at great length. As in the case of the Seventh Special Session, Kissinger produced a speech outlining several thoughts and suggestions on the issues before the Paris conference. He repeated the proposal for the creation of an International Energy Institute that would promote new energy sources in the developing countries. On international monetary reforms, he expressed the hope that many of the proposals mentioned by the United States at the Seventh Special Session would be finally approved at the IMF Meeting in Kingston, and he suggested further activities for the new forum in Paris, in relation to UNCTAD, the General Agreement on Tariffs and Trade (GATT), and the World Food Council.

In other speeches, ministers from Algeria, Iran, and Iraq refuted the view that the rise in oil prices was the principal cause for the worsening of the plight of the poorest, blamed the industrialized countries for the crisis in the international monetary and financial system, and emphasized as the focal point for future negotiations their demand for concessions from the industrial rich.

The developing countries proved to be quite canny in choosing their representatives as cochairmen of the commissions. Aware of the fact that the OPEC countries would be in a much better position to deal with the Western industrialized countries, they let the OPEC ministers take the lead. Apart from Venezuela, which was serving as the cochairman of the conference, Saudi-Arabia, Iran, and Algeria were named as cochairmen of the commissions on energy, finance, and development, respectively. Peru was the only non-OPEC country named to take the developing countries' chair on the raw materials commission. The other side named the United States for energy, Japan for raw materials, and the EEC for both development and finance. The commissions were asked to meet monthly, from mid-February on.

A word about an interesting side issue at the Paris conference. The French president had, in his opening address, talked about the possiblity of involving the USSR and other East European states in the future work of the conference. The participants at the conference also learned that the Russians had complained about their exclusion from the conference. No decisions were taken on this question at the conference, but it was understood that the issue would come up for discussion again in the future.

The commissions began their work in February, but were almost immediately bogged down in technicalities. At a press conference in April 1976, Manuel Perez Guerrero of Venezuela complained of "lack of progress" in Paris.[8] It was assumed at that time that the United States wanted to wait until after UNCTAD IV to resume serious negotiations. These negotiations, which have resumed now, are tough and involved, but there is agreement all around that the Paris commissions provide the best possible framework for discussions and bargaining between the two sides.

How are the negotiations in Paris related to negotiations and developments within the framework of the United Nations? UN Secretary General Kurt Waldheim expressed some anxiety on the subject when he spoke at the Seventh Special Session; and several UN organs and agencies were represented at the Paris conference. Some of the issues that have come up before the commission on financing obviously relate to the work of the World Bank, IMF, and UNCTAD, while the issues being discussed in the commissions on raw materials and development relate closely to the concerns of UNCTAD, FAO, and UNDP. On energy, the UN does not have an active organ; but it is conceivable that the UNEP could begin to take an interest in energy problems as part of its broader environmental concerns.

It would seem that the link between these commissions and the UN system would remain at best an informal one. While the UN would obviously take note of suggestions and recommendations emanating from these commissions, there is no way that their functioning could be related to the formal structure of the UN. The bargaining that went into the creation of these commissions and the hard negotiations that lie ahead within the mandate of each commission are not particularly suited to the style of UN diplomacy; and in some ways, therefore, it would be best to leave these commissions to function on their own while building up and promoting a series of contacts between them and various UN organs and organizations. There is already some evidence of positive interaction between the Paris commissions and the UN system. The Development Commission in Paris urged in March 1976 potential donors to the IFAD to indicate their contributions to the UN secretary general by April 15, 1976, so that the fund could begin to function at an early date.[9] This has already had the desired effect on the potential donors, and the fund was formally launched in June 1976.

UNCTAD IV

After the Seventh Special Session, UNCTAD IV (Nairobi, May 1976) became a focal point for further activities within the UN system. The previous UN Conferences on Trade and Development (Geneva, Delhi, and Santiago) were unable to achieve any substantial results because of the unbridgeable gap between the demands of the Third World on trade and development issues, and the concessions that the industrialized countries were willing to offer. The UNCTAD officials were hopeful that UNCTAD IV would be somewhat more successful. To this end, only eight substantive items were placed on the agenda of UNCTAD IV, contrary to the practice at the previous conferences, where vast numbers of major and minor items were listed for discussion. It was also agreed in advance that while the general debate on the agenda items would take place in the plenary sessions, all negotiations would be conducted in closed sessions. The substantive issues before the conference were, however, not much nearer resolution than they were at the time of the Seventh Special Session; and while the positions of various groups on some of these issues were clarified further, and a vague and general consensus evolved on some other issues, the main thrust of the decisions taken at the conference was to continue the process of negotiations.

The major issue before UNCTAD IV was the situation of the producers of raw materials. References have been made in earlier chapters to the worsening balance-of-payments situation of most of the raw-material-producing countries. Part of this is caused by price fluctuations which relate to boom and slump periods in Western economies. Though some commodities have, because of scarcity of supplies, retained high price levels, many others have suffered from lowering of prices due to depression in the market economies. The other reason for the unfavorable balance-of-payment situation is the inflation in the West and the resultant increase in the prices of manufactured goods and services that the developing countries need to buy. The rising price of oil and food imports and the servicing of debts incurred by the developing countries in earlier years constitute other major problems for the developing countries in this area.

The UNCTAD Integrated Programme for Commodities,[10] elaborated in response to a recommendation of the Sixth Special Session,[11] seeks to provide solutions to these problems on a long-term basis. The program has five key elements:

- establishment of a common fund, which would finance international commodity stocks;
- setting up of international stocks for several commodities;
- improvement and enlargement of facilities for compensatory financing, which would help to offset fluctuations in the export earnings of developing countries;
- multilateral trade commitments on individual commodities;
- removal of trade barriers and other impediments to the expansion of commodity processing capacity in developing countries.

Under the program, UNCTAD proposes the establishment of buffer stocks of key commodities such as copper, bauxite, rubber, tea, coffee, cocoa, sugar, jute, hard fibers, and cotton. Stocks will be released in times of shortages and held back in times of surplus, thus stabilizing supply and demand. The initial cost for purchase and storage of the buffer stocks is estimated around $3 billion.

Following intensive negotiations, UNCTAD IV agreed on a consensus resolution endorsing the Integrated Programme for Commodities.[12] The resolution calls for steps to be taken toward the creation of a common fund, and requests UNCTAD to convene a negotiating conference before March 1977. Noting, at the same time, that "there are differences of views as to the objectives and modalities of a common fund," the resolution proposes preparatory meetings prior to the negotiating conference to study the objectives and financing of the common fund.

The somewhat vague and general text of the resolution reflects the lack of agreement on many of the specific proposals included in the original package. While the Netherlands and Norway had announced their support of the integrated program before the conference, the United States, the United Kingdom, the Federal Republic of Germany, and Japan maintained their reservations on the program until almost the last day of the conference. Following hurried consultations that took place in Germany between U.S. Secretary of State Kissinger and German Chancellor Helmut Schmidt, the United States and the Federal Republic of Germany softened their position; and along with the United Kingdom and Japan agreed to join a consensus to negotiate further on the issues involved.

In a statement issued on May 31, 1976 the chief of the United States delegation, Deputy Secretary of State Charles Robinson, conceded that there might be an advantage in linking individual commodity agreements. However, the United States would decide on its participation in the negotiating conference on the common fund only after studying fully the results of the preparatory conferences. Robinson also ruled out indexation.

Along with negotiations on the common fund, negotiations are to take place on individual commodities. In all cases, preparatory meetings will precede the negotiating conferences, and UNCTAD IV proposed that the individual commodity agreements be finalized "by the end of 1978."[13]

The integrated program calls for enlarged compensatory financing to stabilize the export earnings of commodity producers. In view of the general opposition on the part of the industrialized countries to indexation proposals, compensatory financing would seem to offer the best prospects for stabilizing the earnings of the countries exporting raw materials.

UNCTAD IV called for extending the Generalized Scheme of Preferences (GSP) in favor of developing country exports, and as far as possible, duty-free entry of their manufactures and semimanufactures into developed country markets.[14] Under GSP, which was first negotiated in Tokyo in September 1973 under the auspices of GATT, industrialized countries are expected to grant tariff concessions to developing countries. In order to encourage industrial development in the developing countries, the conference asked the industrialized countries to strengthen and develop policies "that would encourage domestic factors of production to move progressively from the lines of production which are less competitive internationally, especially where the long-term comparative advantage lies in favor of developing countries."[15]

On the problem of debts, the Group of 77 had put forward five major proposals:

1. cancellation of debts owed by the 29 "least developed countries" (LDCs) to industrialized country governments,
2. postponement until 1980 of interest payments and capital repayments of loans owed by the "most seriously affected" countries (MSAs),
3. rescheduling of short-term commercial debts into long-term obligations of 25 years,
4. refinancing of debts owed to international institutions like IMF, and
5. the convening of an international debtor-creditor conference to discuss the entire problem of debts.

The United States and other industrialized countries took the view that action to ease the debt problems could only be taken on a case-by-case basis. But they also indicated their willingness to consider individual requests for debt relief, in a multilateral framework. The proposal for an international conference on debt problems was accepted indirectly, in that appropriate existing international forums were invited to determine before the end of 1976 what features would provide guidance on dealing with debt problems on an individual basis.[16]

Through other resolutions, UNCTAD IV emphasized "collective self-reliance," calling upon developing countries to promote and strengthen economic cooperation among themselves,[17] and asked the East European socialist countries to expand and improve their scheme of generalized preferences vis-à-vis the developing countries.[18]

The main result of UNCTAD IV is that negotiations would continue on the major issues through UNCTAD and UN channels, and also through the Paris talks. An assessment of what could be achieved through such negotiations in the future would lie along the following lines:

1. Though UNCTAD is to continue working on the proposal for a common fund, such a fund is unlikely to be established until the United States and

several other industrialized countries drop their reservations. It has been suggested that OPEC might provide the funds required for setting up of the fund to support buffer stocks. Even if this were possible, the arrangement would not work without the cooperation of the industrialized countries. If the western industrialized countries did not agree to participate in the buffer stock arrangement as envisaged by UNCTAD, they would probably use their own stocks to manipulate supply and demand. Developing countries recognize this reality.

Negotiations on individual commodity agreements will go forward and separate funds may be established to support buffer stocks for many of these commodities. Efforts will be made to establish a link between these funds, in case the establishment of a common fund is delayed.

2. Though the industrialized countries are opposed to indexation, they have shown themselves favorable to the idea of compensatory financing. The Lomé Agreement, which was signed by EEC with 46 developing countries, provides a mechanism for price stabilization and for countries dependent upon export of certain commodities to draw compensation from a fund when their earnings drop below a baseline. This scheme is similar to IMF's compensatory financing scheme. Professor Hans Singer of the Institute of Development Studies, Sussex, feels that this willingness of the industrialized countries to accept the idea of compensation ought to be pursued further, and that other mechanisms could be developed to provide compensatory financing.[19]

3. The Western industrialized countries and Japan should also be willing to support an increase in Third World exports, including manufactured and processed products. GSP, under which tariff concessions are granted to developing countries, is officially a temporary measure—it is to remain in force for ten years. The developing countries would like to see its life extended. They would also like to obtain guarantees against changes in these preferences being brought about by industrialized countries under pressure from their industries during the current economic recession.

4. Further push in the direction of achieving the 0.7 percent target for official aid may also produce results. Several of the European countries have already accepted the target. The United States remains unwilling to accept the target officially, but once the dust of the 1976 presidential elections settles, the United States may move toward increasing its development assistance. OPEC countries have already reached and surpassed the 0.7 percent target. OECD estimates that the official development assistance in 1974 was 1.4 percent of GNP for the aid-giving members of OPEC. OPEC aid commitments in that year came to $5.3 billion and actual transfers to $2.2 billion. This should be compared with the official development assistance provided by the industrialized countries, which came to 0.33 percent of their GNP in 1974. Considerable pressure therefore needs to be exercised on the industrialized countries, from within and without, to bring it up to the 0.7 percent target. However, in the post-Seventh Special Session period, there is a better atmosphere, and greater

willingness on the part of many of these countries to increase aid; and they can be pressed to move further in this direction.

5. There is also the problem of mounting debts for the developing countries. The problem is particularly acute for 88 non-oil-producing countries. Their debt burden is estimated to have doubled between 1970 and 1975, to $135 billion. In 1975, these countries had to find $11.5 billion to cover servicing for their debts, while the assistance they received came to only $9.4 billion.

The United States remains opposed to an across-the-board approach to the problem of debts, but there are some signs that, along with other industrialized countries, it may be willing to discuss a debt moratorium for the group of the poorest countries, and a rescheduling and refinancing of the debts owed by several others.

6. UNCTAD has advocated the formation of producer associations to enable producers of major commodities to coordinate their export policies and prices, and UNCTAD IV provided an opportunity for further discussion on the need for and value of such associations. There are already producer associations for bananas, bauxite, copper, cocoa, rubber, tea, tin, tungsten, phosphates, and coffee; and they are being actively encouraged by UNCTAD as a means of exerting further pressure on market forces from the side of the producers and also increasing their bargaining power vis-à-vis transnational companies.

The United States favors producer-consumer forums (to negotiate on commodity agreements), but seems resigned to the need to also deal with producer associations as they come up.

7. Some of the broader issues that were discussed at UNCTAD IV relate to the need to tailor international and regional assistance plans to the specific needs and requirements of different groups of developing countries. The media jargon already includes "Fourth World" as a term to cover about 40 countries that are the poorest among the developing countries. It is clear that the economic and financial needs of these countries are much more pressing and urgent, and any attempt to deal with their problems will have to take into account this urgency.

WORLD EMPLOYMENT CONFERENCE

Following UNCTAD IV, the World Employment Conference organized by the International Labor Organization (ILO) took place in Geneva from June 4 to 17, 1976. The main objective of the conference was to encourage "the adoption by each country of a basic needs approach, aiming at the achievement of a certain specific minimum standard of living before the end of the century. The main instruments for attaining this goal would be increasing the volume and productivity of employment and taking the national and international measures of economic policy needed to bring this about."[20]

The conference was important in that it drew attention to the need for national action to fulfill basic needs. While most other conferences have dealt with international issues, the ILO conference dealt with national issues, pointing out that transfer of resources from one set of countries to another would itself not be enough unless it were complemented by vigorous national strategies to alleviate poverty. There were differences of opinion on how these national strategies ought to be formulated and implemented, and the program finally adopted by the conference was, as in the case of UNCTAD, a result of fortuitous compromise. Its basic message, however, is quite clear—the importance of each country defining and implementing its own strategy on basic needs.

LOOKING AHEAD

The flurry of international meetings and conferences, which have taken place since the Seventh Special Session and will continue to take place in the months to come, has raised expectations for an early progress on many of the critical issues, expectations that are unlikely to be fulfilled. The process of negotiations on these issues is hard and difficult, and a willingness to break new ground has not yet become evident, at least as far as the major industrialized countries are concerned.

Yet, if the momentum toward finding viable solutions is to be maintained, steady progress will be needed on questions such as the funding and maintenance of commodity buffer stocks, multilateral commodity arrangements, extension of GSP, and compensatory financing or other schemes to help developing countries stabilize their export earnings. Debt rescheduling and, at least in the case of the poorest countries, a debt moratorium will have to be worked out in the near future; and official development assistance will have to rise, not only to keep pace with inflationary trends, but to provide extra resources for development. Provision of additional development capital, through the World Bank and other international and regional institutions, will have to be increased in volume and accelerated. Though the role of private capital will continue to arouse debate and controversy, there are many countries in the developing world which need and would welcome such capital, under suitable guarantees and provisos.

NOTES

1. For detailed information on the decisions taken at these meetings, see IMF, *Summary Proceedings, Annual Meeting 1975,* Washington D.C., 1975; and IBRD, IFC, and IDA, *Summary Proceedings, Annual Meeting 1975,* Washington D.C., 1975.

2. For further information, see IMF Survey, Vol. 5, No. 1, January 5, 1976.

3. For detailed information, see IMF Survey, Vol. 5, No. 2, January 19, 1976.
4. New York *Times,* January 9, 1976.
5. Ibid.
6. New York *Times,* January 10, 1976.
7. UN Doc. A/31/107, June 18, 1976.
8. New York *Times,* April 29, 1976.
9. UN Press release FC/42, March 31, 1976.
10. UNCTAD Doc. TD/184, March 4, 1976.
11. United Nations General Assembly, *Resolution 3202* (S-VI), May 1, 1974.
12. UNCTAD, *Resolution,* TD/RES/93(IV), May 30, 1976.
13. Ibid.
14. UNCTAD, *Resolution,* TD/RES/96(IV), May 31, 1976.
15. Ibid.
16. UNCTAD, *Resolution,* TD/RES/94(IV), May 31, 1976.
17. UNCTAD, *Resolution,* TD/RES/87(IV), May 30, 1976.
18. UNCTAD, *Resolution,* TD/RES/95(IV), May 31, 1976.
19. *The New Internationalist,* April 1976, p. 7.
20. *Employment, Growth and Basic Needs: A One-World Problem* (Geneva: ILO, 1976),
p. 6.

4

Among the problems that the developing countries face today, hunger has become the most important. Progress on various economic and social fronts will be impossible until minimum food needs are met the world over on a continuing, regular basis. Food, shelter, health, education, and employment remain the five major areas of human need, with food obviously coming first.

The current phenomenon of scarce food supplies arises because of a complex set of factors—dwindling food reserves, population growth, greater per capita demand for food among middle classes in the developing countries, and the extremely high consumption rate in the industrialized societies. In 1961, the world food reserves (mostly held by the United States) amounted to 231 million metric tons in grain, equivalent to 105 days' supply of world needs. In 1974, these reserves had declined to a level equivalent to only 33 days' supply; in 1976 they represented scarcely 31 days' supply. Population growth accounts for a steady increase in world demand. There has also been a perceptible increase in per capita food consumption by the middle classes in countries like India and Pakistan, increasing the demand for high calorie food, such as milk and meat products and also cereals. The fourth major factor is the increased per capita consumption in the industrialized societies because of rising affluence.* Whereas in the developing countries the average grain requirement per person is estimated at 400 pounds, most of which is directly consumed to provide minimum food needs, the annual per capita requirement

---

*It is estimated that the demand for cereals is growing at an annual rate of 30 million metric tons, of which 22 million are absorbed by increasing population and 8 million by rising per capita consumption.

in the United States, the USSR, or Canada is almost nearly a ton of grain. Of this, only 200 pounds is consumed directly as bread, breakfast cereal, or pastries; the rest is consumed indirectly in the form of milk, eggs, or meat. Thus, the average grain consumption of a Russian or North American is five times that of an Indian.

Add to these factors vagaries of weather, erratic and chancy market mechanisms, and inadequate internal distribution systems within developing countries, and we get some idea of the seriousness of the food problem today. India, which was nearing self-sufficiency in food supplies in 1971 as a result of the use of fertilizers, better seeds, and better cultivation methods slipped back badly in 1972 and 1973 because of inadequate rains; and toward the end of 1973 the extraordinary rise in the oil import costs compounded its problems further. The inadequate distribution system within the country was regarded as yet another factor responsible for the food crisis that arose in India in 1974. In 1975 and 1976 the weather was more favorable to India, and bumper crops were harvested. India seems once again on the threshold of self-sufficiency. But the only way it can maintain its gains in agricultural production is by continuing to invest heavily in agriculture and by improving its storage facilities and distribution mechanisms.

When the international development strategy for the Second Development Decade was being drafted in 1970, agriculture was given a heavy emphasis. The strategy listed a variety of measures that were needed to improve and increase agricultural production, to expand rural employment, and to increase export earnings. It called for an average annual increase of 4 percent in the agricultural production of the developing countries. The results for the first five years of the decade have, however, been somewhat disappointing. The World Economic Survey of 1975 estimates that the attainment of the objective of a 4 percent annual increase over the decade as a whole would now require an average expansion of 5.5 percent a year during 1976 to 1980. But this seems unlikely. The best that can be expected is 4 percent annual increase in the remaining years of the decade, thus bringing the annual average for the decade as a whole to 3.3 percent. Such a rate of increase would accomodate most of the expansion in demand resulting from population growth, as well as the expected rise in per capita demand.[1]

The pressure exercised by population growth on food supplies provides an extra dimension to the food problem. The number of countries that now have to import food to feed their populations continues to increase year by year. Of the 115 countries for which data are available, all but a few now import grain. These include most of the countries in Europe, Asia, Africa, and Latin America (including such large countries as the USSR and China). The United States and Canada have now emerged as the world's breadbasket.

As Table 2 indicates, grain exports from North America nearly doubled in the years between 1970 and 1976, expanding from 56 million metric tons in 1970 to nearly 94 million metric tons in 1976. For the foreseeable future,

Table 2

The Changing Pattern of World Grain Trade[a]
(million metric tons)

Region	1934–38	1948–52	1960	1970	1976[b]
North America	+ 5	+23	+39	+56	+94
Latin America	+ 9	+ 1	0	+ 4	− 3
Western Europe	−24	−22	−25	−30	−17
Eastern Europe and USSR	+ 5	—	0	0	−27
Africa	+ 1	0	− 2	− 5	−10
Asia	+ 2	− 6	−17	−37	−47
Australia and N.Z.	+ 3	+ 3	+ 6	+12	+ 8

[a] Plus sign indicates net exports; minus sign, net imports.
[b] Preliminary estimates of fiscal year data.
Source: Derived from FAO and USDA data and estimates by Lester R. Brown.

the position of North America in this regard is unlikely to change. Two other countries—Australia and New Zealand—are to be found in the league of net grain exporters, but their exports are expected to be only about 8 million metric tons, down from 12 million metric tons in 1970.

The problem of food scarcity affects the developing countries most severely. For millions of poor people in the developing world, the daily intake of food does not provide the minimum nutritional requirements, even in normal times. And when food shortages occur, these are always the people who suffer most.

An alarming aspect of this problem is malnutrition, which in many cases has a permanent debilitating effect on the young and the adolescent. Retardation and brain damage occur in numerous cases of prenatal malnutrition and insufficient intake of protein during early childhood. In several areas in India, four out of every five preschool children are reported to suffer from dwarfism caused by malnutrition.

More than 15 million children under five die each year because of malnutrition and infection. Of the total number of deaths in the world, this would constitute approximately 25 percent. As the children grow up, the problem of hunger and malnutrition continues to haunt most of them for the rest of their lives.

Increased agricultural production is the only answer to these problems. The Rome World Food Conference, the Seventh Special Session, and the 1975 FAO Assembly all stressed this point. The prospects for increasing agricultural production in the developing countries are not unfavorable. In the years to come, the area of arable land is expected to increase by about 10 million hectares (about 1.5 percent) a year and the area under irrigation by about 4 million hectares (about 6 percent) a year. The use of high-yield varieties, pesticides, and fertilizers can result in enormous gains in productivity. Achievement of such gains will require increasing national investment in agriculture, improvements in storage, distribution, and marketing facilities, development of resources directed toward solving agricultural problems of special interest to developing countries, and increasing international assistance for agricultural projects.

Looking at the next 25 years, there are several areas where needs can be forecast and action suggested:

1. There will be a continuing need for food aid on an emergency basis in situations such as that of Bangladesh and the Sahel area in 1973–74.
2. Food aid will also need to be provided to those countries that suffer from shortages and that are not in a position to provide for their needs with their own foreign exchange earnings. The World Food Conference estimated the annual food aid requirement at 10 million tons. FAO indicates that during 1975–76 actual commitments for food aid came to 9 million tons. The 10 million ton target thus appears to have support.
3. There are countries that will need to import food by paying the regular market price or a price negotiated on mutually satisfactory terms with the exporters.
4. Productivity and output can be increased in many countries through increased supply of pesticides, fertilizers, and better seeds, and through improvements in agricultural methods and techniques.
5. Part of the food problem can be solved by variations in dietary habits with an increase in consumption of those items that are likely to remain available in larger supplies and a decrease in the consumption of those items whose supply cannot be increased much more.

THE POPULATION FACTOR

The relationship of food to population is a crucial factor. Whether we accept the Malthusian theory or not, it remains incontrovertible that all those countries whose population growth is outpacing food supplies will have to undertake urgent measures to bring these two factors into balance in the very near future.

It also needs to be remembered that food scarcity affects the poorer sections of a society most directly and most severely. In Bangladesh, the number and the percentage will be very high; in an oil-producing Arab country like Abu Dhabi, the number may not be very large and the percentage may decline rather rapidly, given the ability of the country to subsidize purchasing power. The fact remains that it is the poor who suffer most in all of these countries. To some extent, this is true even of highly industrialized countries like the United States.

What is needed, as a minimum, is an efficient and equitable distribution policy which will enable food supplies to be rushed to the areas where scarcity occurs, enable everyone to receive the minimum amount of food needed for survival and sustenance, and provide the poor with the means to buy the food required. Though claims of national sovereignty very often preclude any international discussion of internal distribution policies, there may be a need in the future to link international food assistance, not only to tangible evidence of national effort to increase productivity and production, but also to proof of an efficient and equitable distribution system. Otherwise, food aid is likely to benefit mostly those who can afford the prices, that is, the rich and the middle classes.

Rafael M. Salas, who managed the highly successful Green Revolution in the Philippines from 1966 to 1968, and now heads the United Nations Fund for Population Activities (UNFPA), says that an effective management and distribution system is as important as a drive to increase food production. Without an adequate policy and administrative framework, available food supplies may not reach those for whom they are intended, and a good part of it may indeed remain unused or go to waste.

POLITICS OF FOOD

In recent months, discussion of food being used as a political weapon has come up on two levels. The first relates to the so-called "triage theory," which advocates abandoning "basket cases" such as Bangladesh because they will be dependent on external aid to an ever-increasing degree, and who should be left to perish, as international assistance is unlikely to be of much help to them in solving their long-term problems. This theory erroneously assumes that parts of the world can be insulated from the impact of developments—political, economic, or social—in other parts of the world. It should be evident to those who advocate this theory that the idea of abandoning human beings to their own fate on the ground that they can not be helped on a long-term basis is, apart from being inhumane, also impractical. Bangladesh cannot be abandoned, because what happens there will affect neighbouring countries, and then, in ever-widening ripples, all the others. In the second place, though Bangladesh and other countries in that category may not be able to produce enough food for themselves, they are in a position to produce goods that may be able to pay for at least part of the food needed. Their full agricultural potential has yet to be realized, and assistance aimed at increasing their productivity and overall agricultural production may produce increasingly satisfactory results.

At another level, the politics of food concerns the role that North American countries can play in influencing and directing the food supply situation in future. The role of Canada and the United States as global food suppliers which began in the 1940s and continued to expand in the '50s, '60s, and '70s, is likely to expand further. In contrast, the OPEC countries will need more food in the future because of their increasing population and increasing consumption needs. Another group of countries that experimented with the Green Revolution in the late '60s and the early '70s faces the problem of increasing population, and though each one of them is making strenuous efforts to increase its food production, the pressure of population is likely to result in a continuing need for food imports. This group includes countries like Pakistan, Mexico, and Turkey. The USSR continues to depend on imported grain, and so does China, though it is undertaking vigorous action to bring its population in balance with its food resources. Japan will remain an importer on a large scale, as also will many European countries. Given this situation, there are those in the United States who argue that food could be used in the same way as OPEC countries are using oil—as a political weapon.

Others argue for a more constructive approach. Lester Brown suggests that the United States and Canada should form a joint commission on food policy to manage food exports through an international strategy, based on decisions taken at the Rome Food Conference and the Bucharest Population Conference. Under such a strategy, countries that are implementing national programs to bring food and population into balance will be given access to imports in times of scarcities, over and above those who do not follow such programs.[2] Brown says:

> There now exists an opportunity to indicate explicitly that those countries that support the internationally accepted strategy to solve the world food problem through responsible national actions can freely share our food. Those that refuse will receive no such assurance. Those countries in which agriculture is stagnating or lagging will need to reform their agricultural sectors and do whatever is necessary to get production moving. All countries should be required to be explicit about their own food reserve goals and the specific steps they are taking to achieve them. Those countries that are not following the World Plan of Action agreed upon at the UN Population Conference at Bucharest in August of 1974 and are not contributing to the stabilization of world population should not count on access to North American food supplies. In effect, access to North American food supplies should be used as an incentive to encourage and assist countries to do their share in solving the food problem, and thereby to help avoid an unmanageable food crisis.

AN INTERNATIONAL STRATEGY

While it may be useful to form a joint Canadian-U.S. commission, it would be prudent for these two countries to coordinate their export policies with other exporters through international organizations. This will help them to maintain a better worldwide perspective and protect them from the charge that they are using food exports to serve their own political ends.

A further step in the same direction will be to let an organization like the World Food Council decide on and implement a system of guidelines under which countries would receive food supplies. The World Food Conference in November 1974 asked for establishment of international reserves, portions of which will be contributed through creation of national reserves. The World Food Council, as the overseeing authority for those reserves, will be in a good position to compare needs and requirements of different countries, to see what national policies are being followed toward encouraging self-reliance, and to decide how available reserves should be allocated at any given time.

Another element of the international strategy in this area is IFAD. The fund's creation was proposed by the Rome Food Conference, and endorsed by the Seventh Special Session. The fund, with $1 billion as its capital, will provide both grants and loans to countries planning to improve their agricultural production.

In summary, a strategy aimed at dealing with the problem of food supplies in the next 25 years should have the following components:

1. An international reserve system directed by an organization such as the World Food Council which, in addition to coordinating emergency food aid, will seek to direct supplies toward countries in need of imports, preference being given to those that are undertaking vigorous programs to increase agricultural production and to reach a balance between people and resources.
2. An international fund to help countries to improve agricultural methods and to achieve an increase in agricultural production. IFAD is expected to fulfill this role.
3. National programs that aim at exploiting the full potential of food production in the respective countries, that seek to change dietary habits where possible, and that are accompanied by systematic efforts at achieving equitable distribution.

Such a strategy will call for an effort in all countries to slow down population growth, and in the industrialized countries to reduce overconsumption.

What role can the FAO play in promoting such a strategy? FAO, which is one of the oldest organizations in the UN family, has many achievements to its credit; but right now, as Edouard Saouma, its director general, pointed out in an interview,[3] the organization is top-heavy, with a very large bureaucracy based at headquarters and a very high percentage of its budget going into maintenance of its administrative and managerial structure. If FAO is to play a major role in promoting a worldwide food strategy, it would have to cut down on its administrative structure, and be able to provide expertise and technical assistance at the cheapest possible cost to the countries concerned. This may require revising radically the whole concept of technical assistance.

The Consultative Group on Food Production and Investment (CGFPI), which has been set up jointly by FAO, the World Bank, and UNDP, following a recommendation of the Rome Food Conference, has the responsibility for stimulating the flow of resources to developing countries for food production, and promoting bilateral and multilateral aid coordination. The group has already held several meetings, and is expected to become an important coordination instrument.

IFAD is now assured of the contributions required to launch its operations; and with $1 billion in capital, the fund should be able to provide substantial assistance to the countries that have well-defined plans for increasing and improving food production.

The need for close interrelationship between FAO, IFAD, the World Food Council, and other concerned organizations is obvious. The council, organized as an interministerial body, will have the political role of overseeing developments in the field, with IFAD providing funds, and FAO technical assistance. The complex institutional framework can be made to work; but this will require imaginative and decisive leadership in all the organizations, and a flexible approach on their part to program needs.

NOTES

1. *UN World Economic Survey, 1975,* E/5790/Add.1.

2. Lester R. Brown, *The Politics and Responsibility of the North-American Breadbasket* (Washington, D.C.: Worldwatch Institute, 1975), p. 41.

3. New York *Times,* April 25, 1976.

5

The world population reached 4 billion at the end of 1975; and the latest UN projections are that it will go up to 6.25 billion by the year 2000.[1] During the past 15 years, the interrelationship of population growth with food supplies, housing needs, educational planning, employment policies, urbanization, and the use of resources, has been seen much more clearly than before; and both pessimistic and optimistic views have emerged as to the impact of future population growth on human well-being. On balance, it is possible to argue today that the optimists have the better case.

FOOD AND POPULATION

The food-population equation, which was briefly touched on in the previous chapter, remains the most discussed of these interrelationships. As Figure 1 shows, total food production in the developing countries taken as a whole has risen considerably between 1960 and 1975. But population growth also has been quite rapid; and the per capita food production has not increased very much. Given variable harvests, uneven supply and distribution problems, most developing countries have had to import food; and during the mid-sixties and again in 1972–73 serious shortages occurred in South Asia. The early seventies were also marked by a severe crisis in the Sahel region of Africa. Though famine was eventually averted through emergency aid, food shortage continues to plague a large part of the developing world; and recent problems with energy and fertilizer supply have affected the food production prospects in many countries.

There is a clear case for increased investment in food production and agricultural development, and both national and international efforts are under way to meet this need. But as UNFPA executive director Rafael M. Salas pointed out at the 1974 World Food Conference:

> The measures called for to cope with ... immediate problems of feeding the large population cannot be continued indefinitely. It is therefore essential ... also to look at the long-range relationships between population growth and food supply beyond 1985. All governments should consider realistically their long-term requirements for food and other basic necessities against the background of their natural resources and the availability of means—human, technological, institutional and financial—for utilizing them and adopt consistent with their needs and goals, the appropriate population policies and programmes.[2]

The broader equation between population and resources has also been a subject of much debate in recent years. Paul and Anne Ehrlich have vigorously argued for stringent limitations on population growth, on the grounds that "Spaceship Earth is now filled to capacity or beyond and is running out of food,"[3] that many mineral resources are nonrenewable, and that there are foreseeable limits on the use of all other resources which are needed to sustain

FIGURE 1
Food and Population in Developing Countries, 1960–75

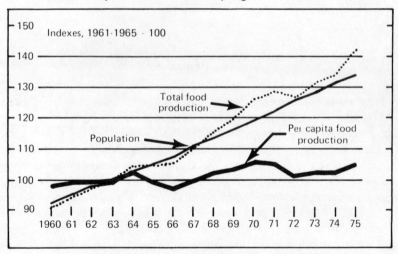

Note: Data for noncommunist countries.
Source: Economic Research Service, USDA.

human life. Paul Ehrlich's view, since he wrote *The Population Bomb* has been that population control measures need to be undertaken immediately; otherwise disaster looms ahead. He has now somewhat modified his view, in that he recognizes that economic and social development needs to accompany efforts to stabilize population growth. He remains, however, an ardent advocate of population control measures.

The Club of Rome's report on *Limits to Growth* also saw disaster ahead, because of rapid population growth, depletion of finite resources, and despoliation of environment. In its more recent report, *Mankind at the Turning Point,* the Club of Rome retreats from this dire prognosis, declaring that planned "organic growth" which avoids environmental and other dangers is the answer. The club, however, remains concerned with the threat of rapid population growth.

Lester Brown, in his book, *In the Human Interest,* outlines a population stabilization strategy (see Table 3), because he also is of the view that finite resources of the Earth cannot support an ever-expanding population. Under the timetable proposed by him, "substantial declines in birth rates between 1975 and 1985 in both the developed and less developed countries, as the former group moved to population stability and the latter lowered their crude birth rate to 25, would reduce the annual world population growth rate from 1.9 per cent in 1970 to 1.1 percent in 1985. This decade would be one of steadily declining fertility throughout the world."[4]

He foresees little further decline between 1985 and 2000 as the population in the developed countries would have already been stabilized, while the young people born during 1960–75 in the developing countries would be in their prime reproductive years. "The second phase of the push toward stabilization would come during the decade from 2005 to 2015, when the sharply reduced group born after 1985 would be entering the prime reproductive years. This would yield a stabilized world population of just under 6 billion by 2015. Even

TABLE 3
A Proposed Population Stabilization Timetable

	1970	1975	1985	2000	2005	2015
World population (billions)	3.6	3.9	4.5	5.3	5.5	5.8
Annual growth rate (percent)	1.9	1.7	1.1	1.0	.9	0
Annual increase (millions)	69	65	50	52	49	0

Source: Lester R. Brown, *In the Human Interest.*

with these extraordinary efforts, the 1970 world population would have increased by nearly two-thirds."[5]

Lester Brown had proposed this timetable prior to the World Population Conference in 1974; and he and many others like him had hoped that the conference would adopt worldwide targets for reduction of birthrates. This did not happen. The World Population Plan of Action adopted by the Bucharest Conference notes "that population growth rates in the developing countries as a whole may decline from the present level of 2.4 per cent per annum to about 2 per cent by 1985; and below 0.7 per cent per annum in the developed countries. In this case the worldwide rates of population growth would decline from 2 per cent to about 1.7 per cent."[6] The plan does not set any worldwide targets for further reductions in the growth rate. It does suggest that "countries which consider their birth rates detrimental to their national purposes are invited to consider setting quantitative goals and implementing policies that may lead to the attainment of such goals by 1985."[7]

The refusal of the Bucharest Conference to set targets for the lowering of birthrates was probably due to national sensitivities regarding outside interference in their population policies; and should not be viewed as a lack of interest on the part of developing countries in the urgency of their population problems.

The post-Bucharest scheme, in fact, provides reasons for cautious optimism. Almost all the Asian countries are already implementing policies aimed at reducing population growth; and many Latin American and Caribbean countries are moving in the same direction. Even in Africa, the number of countries which intend to work out a rational equation between population and resources is growing.

Equally significant is the evidence of a steady downward trend in population growth. A recent study conducted by the Office of Population of the U.S. Agency for International Development (AID) suggests that the world population growth is not as rapid as the UN estimates indicate.[8] The Bucharest Plan of Action had noted a UN projection of 1.7 percent growth in 1985. The U.S. study concludes that the world population growth rate has already declined to 1.63. The study indicates that the annual increase in world population, which was 66 million in 1965, peaked at 70 million in 1970 and then started to decline. By 1974, the annual increase was down to 63 million. Dr. Ray Ravenholt, the director of the AID Office of Population, who reported these findings, believes that an accelerating downward trend is now established, and with a vigorous family planning effort in the next ten years, the growth rate could come down to below 1 percent by 1985. "If this is accomplished then the world population total should be less than 5.5 billion by the year 2000."[9]

These projections, though based on admittedly incomplete data, are startling, particularly if we remember that many people are still talking about a world population of 7 billion in the year 2000. More cautious demographers and family planners will probably disagree with Dr. Ravenholt's projections, and may find the UN figure of 6.25 billion for the year 2000 more reliable. In any case, the demographic transition seems to be occurring sooner than most people had expected or dared to hope.

China

The cases of three countries are cited here to illustrate the efforts undertaken by developing countries to reduce population growth. Two of these—China and India—are the most populous countries in the world, and the population policies they are embarked on will have a significant impact on the world population scene. The population of China was estimated at 823 million in mid-1975. This shows an increase of 240.4 million from the figure of 582.6 million established in 1953. Though exact figures on birth and death rates in China are not available, most demographers agree that there has been a substantial decline between 1965 and 1975. In 1965 the birthrate is estimated to have been around 33 to 35 per thousand, while the death rate was approximately 15 to 17 per thousand. Leon Bouvier of the Population Reference Bureau estimates that by 1975 the birthrate had come down to 25 per thousand, while the death rate was in the vicinity of 10 per thousand.[10] Dr. Ray Ravenholt's estimates are even lower. He believes that the birthrate in China had declined to 14 per 1000 in 1975, while the death rate was 6 per 1000. This would mean an annual growth rate of .80 percent, or an annual population increase of only 7 million.

The Chinese do not advocate population control; but believe in "birth planning" and are making a consistent effort to reduce fertility. The most important elements in this effort are late marriages, easy availability of contraception and "birth planning" services, and a strong motivation program. The minimum age of marriage in China was set in 1950 at 18 for women and 20 for men. Chairman Mao later asked that women postpone marriage until the age of 23, and men until after 26. Though this is not incorporated in law, it is known that both men and women try to adhere to this advice. The family planning program in China is considered among the most effective in the world.

The Chinese experience must be seen, not only in the context of the success of the fertility reduction measures in a highly organized society, but also in the broader context of the socioeconomic measures that have been undertaken to meet basic needs of the entire population.

India

In the case of India, the official population policy has not yet produced the desired results. But it is interesting to note that many of the measures now being introduced in India to meet quantitative targets by 1985, are similar to those adopted in China.

India's population stands today at 600 million. Since 1947, the population has grown by 250 million; and the average monthly increase is now one million. If the population were to continue growing at the present rate, it will reach 1 billion by the end of the century.

The rapid rate of population growth in India is negating in many ways the results of economic and social progress achieved in the last 25 years; and though India was one of the first countries in the world to establish a national population policy, it has not succeeded so far in achieving a very significant reduction in population growth.

India has therefore decided to undertake much stronger measures now, in order to bring its birthrate down from 35 per thousand in 1975 to 25 per thousand in 1985. The age of marriage is to be raised to 18 for females and 21 for males. This should help to prevent early pregnancies, and to increase the age-gap between generations. Female education is to be given increased attention, and child nutrition programs are to receive larger support.

While outlining these policies in an official statement on April 16, 1976, Dr. Karan Singh, the Indian minister of health and family planning, also clarified the government's policy on the much-discussed question of compulsory sterilization.[11] While the central government does not plan to bring in legislation for this purpose, "at least for the time being," state legislators may pass legislation on compulsory sterilization, if they feel the time is ripe. The central government's advice to the states concerned will be to bring in the limitation after three children, and to apply it to all Indian citizens resident in the state.

In order to avoid political squabbles, the Indian government has decided that the representation in the Indian Parliament and the state legislatures will be frozen on the basis of the 1971 census until the year 2001. Moreover, in the allocation of financial assistance to states, where population is a factor, the population figures of 1971 will continue to be followed until the year 2001.

India is the first country in the world to consider compulsory sterilization. The proposal raises serious moral and social issues. There is the additional question whether it can be enforced in practice. There are many who believe that if development efforts keep up their pace, and if the family planning program is implemented vigorously, India may not have to resort to such extreme measures as compulsory sterilization.

Some of the other measures—raising the age of marriage, raising the level of female education, and a scheme of incentives and disincentives—are being used in other countries. Singapore was in fact the first country in Asia to adopt a comprehensive scheme of incentives and disincentives; and in addition to India, several other Asian countries (for example, Pakistan, the Philippines, and the Republic of Korea) have adopted similar schemes.

Mexico

While China and India have had official population programs for more than 20 years, Mexico—which provides our third case history—is a country whose population policy is of very recent origin. Mexico's population in mid-1975 was 60.1 million, up from 42.9 million in 1965. At 3.5 percent, Mexico's population growth rate is one of the highest in the world. Until the end of the sixties, the government was opposed to establishing an official population policy. However, in the early seventies, a private group was allowed to open several family planning clinics. In April 1972, the Mexican government announced that family planning would be integrated with health services, and in November 1973, a new population law was adopted, "with the object of regulating the growth structure, dynamics and distribution of the population, so as to enable the population to benefit fully and equitably from the benefits of economic and social progress."[12]

The law emphasizes the rights of the family and the importance of planned parenthood. Through the National Population Council, established to implement the provisions of the law, Mexico has now rapidly moved to expand the network of service facilities and to inform and educate the Mexican population through the use of public media. The Mexican policy has been given a boost by the declaration of the Roman Catholic Bishops in 1973 that the decision on responsible parenthood is for each couple to make. In a country that is predominantly Roman Catholic, such a declaration is bound to carry great weight. While expanding its population program, Mexico continues to emphasize that the program is not a substitute for economic development.

Mexico is one of the many countries where fertility reduction programs are being developed. There are already several countries (Singapore, Sri Lanka, Hong Kong, the Republic of Korea, Mauritius, Egypt, Trinidad-Tobago, Barbados, Chile, and Costa Rica) where national population policies have helped to reduce population growth significantly, in the last ten to fifteen years. In ten years' time, many other countries may be able to report similar progress.

In all those cases where fertility reduction measures have achieved results, it is recognized that availability of services is only one of the ingredients. Literacy, education, increasing employment of women, and rapid economic and social progress linked to a rise in the general standard of living and assurance of personal economic security provide the other ingredients for the success of the program.

UNFPA

Multilateral assistance for population activities has been channeled through the UNFPA, which began its operations at the end of 1969. UNFPA had disbursed more than $250 million by the end of 1975 for population activities in developing countries and is considered one of the fastest-growing technical assistance programs in the UN system. Its funds have been used to support data collection, policy formulation, family planning, research, training, education and communication programs. Family planning now consumes more than 40 percent of its annual program budget, which stood at $90 million in 1976 and is expected to go up to $95 million in 1977.

UNFPA has sought successfuly to promote worldwide awareness and understanding of the population question, through World Population Year and follow-up activities. It has helped to initiate population programs in a large number of developing countries and is continuing to assist them, in order to sustain their momentum. However, probably the most important contribution that UNFPA has made so far is to bring population within the framework of development planning, and to provide many developing countries with the wherewithal to develop this link. UNFPA can be expected to grow further, given its record and given the demonstrated need for continuing population assistance through multilateral channels.

POPULATION AND DEVELOPMENT

Population programs are a necessity in many developing countries; but in order to be successful, they need to form part of a broad-based development strategy. This was essentially the message of the Bucharest Conference. Professor Hans Singer points out that "the type of government that is active and successful in bringing about direct development (specifically a reduction of poverty) will also be the kind of government that is likely to be active in population control."[13]

The development needs and requirements of the developing countries bring us back to the question of access to and availability of resources. The oft-repeated example of a North American child consuming 40 times more than his Indian counterpart illustrates the point that population growth in the Third World is not the only cause, or even the major cause, for the increasing pressure on world resources. Careless and extravagant use of resources in the industrialized countries is a far more important cause; significant reduction in the use of world resources by the industrialized countries should therefore be considered as important an objective as reduction of population growth in the Third World. "Since a lack of resources for full human development is, as the Bucharest Conference on Population clearly recognized, one of the continuing causes of explosive population growth, to deprive nations of the means of development directly exacerbates their demographic problems."[14] Why should the rich be permitted to use up such a large share of the world's resources, when many of these are finite and are needed in many cases by the poor to break out of the vicious circle of poverty? Why should the Americans, who constitute only 5 percent of the world's population, continue to consume one-third of the available energy and minerals? These questions, which were first raised at the Stockholm Conference on Environment and again at the Bucharest Conference on Population, will be asked, more and more frequently, by the representatives of the developing countries. They can also point out now that the "population explosion" in the developing countries, which has caused so much panic and despair in the West, is, after all, not so much of a crisis, and that it is being brought under control. On the other hand, is there any tangible evidence that the use of resources is being reduced and rationalized in the industrialized countries?

Those, in the West, who argue quite cogently and logically for population stabilization, must, in deference to the same logic, also work for an equitable distribution of the world's resources among the developed and the developing countries.

NOTES

1. United Nations Doc. ESA/P/WP.60, October 6, 1975.

2. Rafael M. Salas, *Food: The Population Factor* (New York: UNFPA, 1974), pp. 1–2.

3. Paul R. Ehrlich and Anne M. Ehrlich, *Population, Resources, Environment* (San Francisco: W. H. Freeman, 1970), p. 3.

4. Lester R. Brown, *In the Human Interest* (New York: W. W. Norton, 1974), pp. 157–158.

5. Ibid., p. 158.

6. United Nations, *World Population Plan of Actions,* CESI/WPY.22, November 1974, para. 16.

7. Ibid., p. 37.

8. Ray Ravenholt, *World Population Crisis and Action Toward Solution,* statement before the U.S. House Appropriations Committee, April 7, 1976, p. 10.

9. Ibid., p. 12.

10. *World Population Growth and Response* (Washington, D.C.: Population Reference Bureau, 1976), p. 76.

11. Dr. Karan Singh, *Statement on National Population Policy,* New Delhi, April 16, 1976.

12. *La Revolución Demografica* (Mexico: Fundación para Estudios de Población, 1975), Ley General de Población, Art. I, translated from the Spanish, p. 125.

13. Hans W. Singer, "Population and Development," *International Development Review,* Washington, D.C., No. 4, 1975, p. 43.

14. Cocoyoc Declaration, UN Doc. A/C.2/292, November 1, 1974.

CHAPTER

6

**TOOLS FOR
CHANGE**

Only 7 percent of the world's industry is located in the developing countries today. Under the plans for a new international economic order, the developing countries want 25 percent of the world industry located in their territories by the year 2000. Why is such a redistribution needed? Is it feasible?

The developing countries that are engaged in commodity trade want to establish processing capacity in their own territories, so that they can acquire a greater share of the wealth generated by commodity trade. Those developing countries that have mineral resources want to be able to exploit them for their own benefit, and those among them that already have significant industrial capacity want to expand this capacity further.

These are some of the reasons behind the insistence of the developing countries that their industrial capacity be expanded. The belief that industry is the key to modernization has sometimes, in a country like India, placed a distorted emphasis on industrial growth, compared to growth in the agricultural sector. The earlier five-year plans in India gave much more importance to industry than to agriculture, and it is only recently that the emphasis has shifted to agriculture.

There is also the tendency on the part of some developing countries to acquire a steel mill or a car manufacturing plant as a showcase, though there may be no appreciable demand for the products of the plant in the countries concerned. Newspapers have occasionally reported cases of imported machinery being allowed to rust and decay, because in their undue haste to acquire the machinery, the countries concerned had not bothered to train personnel who would know how to use and maintain the machinery.

But such extravagant showmanship or waste is not typical of the developing countries, and a reasoned case can be made for rapid industrialization in many of the developing countries. The benefits that will flow from industrialization can be assessed on the basis of verifiable data on available resources and commercially acceptable projections on trade and export potentials.

There is also the natural desire on the part of the developing countries to ensure "control over their natural resources and the exploitation of these natural resources as well as the full utilization of human and material potential at their disposal."[1]

The Declaration and World Plan of Action, adopted at the Second General Conference of UNIDO in Lima in March 1975, stresses the need for urgent industrial development in developing countries, endorsing at the same time the principle of permanent national sovereignty over natural resources.[2]

The principle of permanent national sovereignty over natural resources (with the right to nationalize), which has caused so much debate, was first enunciated in the Charter of Economic Rights and Duties of States drawn up by a group of 40 UN member countries under UNCTAD auspices, at the behest of Lic. Luis Echeverria Alvarez, president of Mexico.[3] President Echeverria had hoped that the charter would gain the unanimous endorsement of the General Assembly, and, like the Declaration on Human Rights, become a point of reference for future agreements on economic relations between states. The charter was adopted at the 29th General Assembly, with 120 votes in favor, six against (including the United States), and ten abstentions.[4] The principle of permanent national sovereignty and the role of transnational corporations were two of the more important points which prevented the emergence of a consensus.

The controversy over these points is unlikely to be resolved in the near future. But, in the meantime, there is a growing trend in the developing countries toward further industrial development. The process of industrialization in large developing countries like India, Pakistan, Mexico, Argentina, and Brazil continues to accelerate. Among the factors which have helped this process are large reserves of natural resources, increasingly skilled manpower, governmental policies in support of industrial development, and large internal markets to absorb a major part of their industrial output. There has been an increasing emphasis, at the same time, on the growth of export-oriented industries. Though the increase in oil prices threw the industrial growth of many of these countries out of kilter, it is likely to pick up again in the near future.

This group of countries includes both low-income and middle-income developing countries. Another group, which has now become engaged in a process of rapid industrialization, includes the middle- and higher-income countries which have benefited from the rise in oil prices. Many of the OPEC countries are investing in hydrocarbon and energy-intensive industries, and countries like Iran, Venezuela, and Nigeria are going all-out to achieve industrial development and diversification, before their oil resources run out.

At the other end of the spectrum, there are many countries dependent on commodity trade, which have limited industrial potential because of lack of natural resources and trained manpower. Many of these countries are in

Africa; and the overall industrial growth is likely to be slow in Africa, certainly slower than that in Latin America and Asia.

The rate of industrial growth in various parts of the Third World will thus be uneven and will depend on both internal and external factors. Though each country will have to work out its policies in the light of its own needs, it is clear that in a large number of developing countries which have not fully utilized either their agricultural or industrial potential there will have to be a balanced development in both sectors. Decentralized development, based on labor-intensive techniques, will help simultaneous growth in various regions, including the rural areas. The generation of greater productive employment must be one of the major aims of industrial development, as most developing countries have large numbers of unemployed and underemployed. In the absence of income-distribution policies motivated by broad concepts of social justice, most of the benefits of rapid industrial growth are likely to accrue to a small group of entrepreneurs at the top. A balance will therefore need to be struck between policies that provide incentives for investment and rapid growth and those that seek to narrow the gap between the rich and the poor. A conscious effort to increase and strengthen women's participation in the labor force will also be required in order to promote broad-based economic and social development.

It is becoming clear that environmental considerations cannot be ignored by developing countries, as industrial progress brings in its wake sprawling urbanization. Issues relating to pollution control, conservation, and appropriate development of resources do not command the same kind of attention in the developing countries as they do in most of the industrialized countries. There are indeed some Third World countries which seem to place exaggerated emphasis on rapid industrial growth, to the virtual exclusion of any consideration of its long-term impact on the quality of life of their people. It is, however, encouraging to note that intelligent and far-sighted planners in many parts of the Third World are beginning to see the need to learn from the environmental experiences of the industrialized countries. The plans and targets for industrial growth set by individual developing countries will thus depend to some extent on how conscious their planners are of environmental considerations.

The external factors that will influence industrial growth in the developing countries are availability of bilateral and multilateral aid and investment, transfer and development of appropriate technology, access to industrial countries' markets, and increasing cooperation among developing countries themselves and between the developing countries and the socialist countries.

Increase in official development assistance, increasing private foreign investment in those countries that want it, and expansion in the operations of the World Bank group and other similar international institutions will help to spur industrial growth in the developing countries. The poorer countries will, of course, need special assistance. During 1969 to 1973 their average GNP growth was about 3 percent, with per capita income increasing by less than 1 percent. In 1974, their GNP growth came down to 2.5 percent, which meant no increase in per capita income at all. The World Bank estimates that if the poorer countries are to achieve average growth of total GNP of at least 4.5 percent—generating a 2 percent per capita income—over 1976 to 1980, the total flow of external financial resources to them would have to go up from the 1974-75 estimated average annual level of $5 billion to $7.5 to $8.5 billion during the coming years.[5]

Industrial growth in many developing countries may one day be further spurred by the changes in the Law of the Sea, which are under negotiation at the UN Law of the Sea Conference. The proposed changes will extend territorial waters from 3 to 12 nautical miles, and establish an exclusive economic zone extending up to 200 nautical miles, under the jurisdiction of coastal states. An International Seabed Authority (ISA) will be established to provide international management of seabed mineral resources. Agreement on the proposed treaty on the law of the sea is being held up because of the deadlock between the coastal states, on the one side, and the land-locked countries and others with inadequate coastlines, on the other. Interestingly, these coalitions cut across the traditional division between the developed and the developing countries.

If and when a new treaty on the law of the sea comes into effect, it is expected that it will give a tremendous fillip to exploration of mineral resources in the exclusive economic zones by governments as well as private companies and transnational corporations, and through contracts and profit-sharing schemes may provide extra resources for industrial growth. The revenues gained by the International Seabed Authority could also be used to assist developing countries in this area.

It has been suggested that a reduction in the military budgets of the developing countries could provide extra resources for development. Similarly, arms reduction policies in the industrialized countries could release substantial capital equipment and technology for peaceful purposes, including assistance for development. These possibilities are, of course, tied to the discussions on arms reduction, some of which are taking place within the UN framework. The East European socialist states have always argued for arms reduction, but negotiations on this question have not yet yielded any practical results. The pursuit of arms reduction goals, though somewhat idealistic at the moment, should not be abandoned, as it may one day yield extremely positive results.

Transfer of appropriate technology, which is dealt with in greater detail in a later section, is another critical factor in the industrial growth of the developing countries. Development of indigenous technology is a complementary priority for developing countries. The UN established in 1971 a World Plan of Action on Science and Technology, which provided a set of guidelines for developing countries to identify their priorities in science and technology.[6] Nothing much has come of it yet. A UN Conference on Science and Technology is now planned for 1979, with the objective of strengthening the technological capacity of developing countries.[7]

Access to industrial countries' markets through the Generalized Scheme of Preferences (GSP) may promote rapid growth of export-oriented industries in the Third World. This has proved to be one of the most difficult areas for negotiations, given the current period of recession in many industrialized countries and the fear of competition from imports, which is shared by the industries and the trade unions in these countries. Yet progress is essential if the developing countries are to achieve their targets of industrial growth; and, more important for the industrialized countries, if they are to continue expanding their exports. The OECD 1975 review of Development Cooperation says, "Experience indicates that as countries industrialize, the already industrialized economies typically gain more markets than they lose."[8]

At the moment, developing countries exchange among themselves only about 20 percent of their exports and imports; 75 percent of their trade is with the industrialized countries, and 5 percent with the socialist countries. The Manila meeting of the Group of 77 accepted the proposal for establishing a program of economic cooperation among developing countries; what is needed now is a detailed strategy that could be implemented in stages. Areas of cooperation that have already emerged need to be strengthened—bilateral ventures among developing countries, financial aid by oil-exporting states to other developing countries, formation of producers' associations and marketing schemes, and emergence of transnational enterprises in the Third World in such fields as aviation, shipping, insurance, and banking.

Shipping is a particularly important area of concern to the developing countries pursuing industrialization, as most of their imports and exports are carried by shipping companies which operate as international cartels in fixing freight rates or handling charges. Since 1971 there has been a sharp increase in liner freight rates as well as in the insurance costs, which cover shipping risks. These need to be regulated and controlled, so as to minimize the net outflow of foreign exchange from developing countries on shipping and insurance accounts. Further development of their own merchant marines by the developing countries through subregional and regional schemes where necessary may provide the long-term answer.

In recent years, socialist countries have provided increasing assistance to a selected group of developing countries (Iran, Afghanistan, India, and several Arab countries) to help their industrial growth; but the total volume remains rather small. Intensification of economic relations between the socialist countries of Eastern Europe and the developing countries will further the goals of industrialization pursued by the developing countries.

TRANSFER OF TECHNOLOGY

The economic growth of developing countries requires adaptation and use of scientific knowledge and information, and of rapidly growing technological know-how. The Green Revolution in Mexico, India, Pakistan, and the Philippines provides an example of successful adaptation of scientific knowledge and know-how to local conditions and needs. The rapid industrial growth in the last two decades in India, Pakistan, Mexico, Argentina, and Brazil came about because of the exploitation of the industrial potential, with the aid and use of modern technology.

Transfer of technology raises many urgent issues. Ninety-five percent of modern technology was originally patented in the industrialized countries, and the rights of ownership and control reside very often in the large, transnational corporations. These corporations also own the vast majority of patents registered in the developing countries, and the royalties charged for their use as well as the costs of technical services provided by the transnationals are generally high. The UNCTAD Secretariat estimates that at the end of the sixties, the foreign exchange costs for developing countries for use of patents, licenses, know-how, and trade marks came to about $1.5 billion, and these costs would probably grow sixfold in the seventies.

One way of measuring the technology gap is to look at the number of scientists and technologists working in the developing countries. To quote UNCTAD estimates, in 1970 there were 112 scientists and engineers per 10,000 population in the industrialized countries, as against 69 for Latin America, 22 for Asia, and only 6 for Africa. The gap is even wider in the field of research and development. The industrialized countries have 10.4 scientists and engineers per 10,000 population working on research and development, while Latin America has 1.15, Asia 1.6, and Africa only 0.35. This problem is compounded by the continuing emigration of skilled personnel from developing to developed countries.[9]

Developing countries therefore attach great importance to the need for transfer of appropriate technology which would help accelerate their development. The question as to how technology can be transferred to developing countries is of course closely related to another question—what kind of technology is most appropriate and suited to local conditions? The establishment of an ultramodern steel mill, with push-button techniques, in an area where there is a very large number of unemployed, does not make much sense, as India found out a few years ago. Should manufacture of synthetics be promoted if this is going to cause problems for producers of raw materials? Should transfer of secondhand plants from developed to developing countries be permitted in order to further industrialization goals and to promote employment, even if this means accelerating environmental despoliation?

There are no easy answers to these questions. But everybody seems to agree now on one thing: labor-intensive technology, which generates large-scale employment, is much more appropriate for developing countries. The World Economic Survey, 1974, points out that this does not necessarily involve the revival of older methods once practiced in industrialized countries but rather the development of labor-intensive technologies of a modern type.[10]

The Programme of Action on the Establishment of a New International Economic Order[11] (see Appendix A) asks for the formulation of "an international code of conduct for the transfer of technology corresponding to the needs and conditions prevalent in developing countries." Draft outlines of such a code were discussed at UNCTAD IV, but the conference did not take a final decision. The Group of 77 would like to see the adoption of a legally binding code; the industrialized countries want the code to be voluntary. The conference agreed to establish an intergovernmental group of experts which "shall be free to formulate draft provisions ranging from mandatory to optional without prejudice to the final decision on the legal character of the code of conduct." The General Assembly was asked to convene a conference under UNCTAD auspices by the end of 1977 to negotiate on the drafts produced by this group of experts and take final decisions.[12]

Another resolution of UNCTAD IV focuses on the need to review and revise the international patent system to meet the special needs of the developing countries.[13] The Group of 77 would like to see the international patent system revised in such a way that the developing countries would be able to use patented processes, relevant to their needs, at nominal charges. The industrialized countries are not willing to go so far, though they would support liberalized access to patents. Kissinger, in his speech to UNCTAD IV, proposed the establishment of an International Industrialization Institute, which would develop and expand research in technology "appropriate to the needs of developing countries" and also run technical training programs.[14]

International action on transfer of technology, including a revision of the patent system, is bound to be slow, as numerous private interests with strong support within the industrialized countries are involved. Whatever international action is eventually agreed upon will have to be accompanied by national action, through new domestic legislation, or the revision of current legislation on the subject.

TRANSNATIONAL CORPORATIONS

A relevant, and equally complex, issue is the role of transnational corporations in the developing countries. The Programme of Action on the Establishment of a New International Economic Order (see Appendix A) calls for an international code of conduct for transnational corporations:

(a) To prevent interference in the internal affairs of the countries where they operate and their collaboration with racist regimes and colonial administrations;

(b) To regulate their activities in host countries, to eliminate restrictive business practices and to conform to the national development plans and objectives of developing countries, and in this context facilitate, as necessary, the review and revision of previously concluded arrangements;

(c) To bring about assistance, transfer of technology and management skills to developing countries on equitable and favourable terms;

(d) To regulate the repatriation of the profits accruing from their operations, taking into account the legitimate interests of all parties concerned;

(e) To promote reinvestment of their profits in developing countries.[15]

Several organizations are now studying the role of transnational corporations. ILO has published several studies on labor relations in transnational corporations, and there is talk of establishing some guidelines on this particular topic. The Lima Conference of UNIDO endorsed the right of states to nationalize transnational corporations in accordance with their own laws, and not under internationally negotiated obligations (which is what the industrialized countries had argued for). Discussions at UNCTAD IV also focused on many aspects of the role of transnational corporations, particularly restrictive business practices.

The UN now has a Centre and a Commission on Transnational Corporations, and both of these bodies are working on a code of conduct. In the meantime, OECD has drafted its own code, which it would like transnationals to observe.[16] The code calls on governments to treat the transnationals as far as possible on the same basis as local companies. At the same time, it set out a number of obligations for the transnationals. They are asked to publish at least once a year detailed financial statements covering their international operations, and also each of their country operations. Such statements should include pertinent information on their shareholdings; principal activities, operating results and sales, and significant new capital investment by geographical areas; and research and development expenditure for the enterprise as a whole.

The code further calls on transnational enterprises not to render any bribe or other improper benefit to any public servant or holder of public office, not to make political contributions unless legally permitted, and to abstain from any improper involvement in local political activities.

OECD plans to establish an intergovernmental group which would, from time to time, review the performance of transnationals under the code and pass judgements; these, however, would not be legally binding. The code is unlikely to satisfy developing countries, but as OECD is apt to point out, three-quarters of transnationals' activities are in the industrialized countries.

The UN system will probably produce and eventually endorse its own code of conduct for transnational corporations. But a period of hard bargaining lies ahead, as the more conservative industrialized countries, particularly the United States and the Federal Republic of Germany, hold views on nationalization and compensation that are diametrically opposed to those of the more militant members of the Group of 77, particularly the Latin Americans. The recent spate of disclosures about overseas payments made by the transnationals, and the shock waves it has created both in the United States and in the countries where payments were allegedly made to politicians, civil servants, and influence-peddlers may make it harder for the United States and other countries not to accept some international regulation of the transnationals; and an international anti-bribery pact may indeed come about earlier than a comprehensive code of conduct for transnational corporations.

There are regional institutions outside the UN framework, which are active on the question of transnationals. One of the latest is the Latin American Economic System (LAES) established in October 1975 at the encouragement of the presidents of Mexico and Venezuela. LAES is to promote the establishment of Latin American transnational corporations; one of these called the Naviera del Caribe has already been created. The other main goals of LAES can be summarized as follows: "to improve the bargaining power of the participant states in order to obtain and utilize capital goods and technology; to establish a common position in negotiations with transnational corporations for the purpose of achieving a just and rational form of cooperation; and to sponsor the organizing of raw material producers' associations as well as the processing of raw materials and resources of the region."[17]

INSTITUTIONAL FRAMEWORK

The Group of 77 considers the UN Industrial Development Organization (UNIDO) the linch-pin of a concerted international effort to promote and accelerate industrial development in the Third World. The Lima Conference recommended that UNIDO become a full-fledged specialized agency of the United Nations, and along with a new Industrial Development Fund, undertake the central coordinating role in changing the world industrial map.[18] This recommendation was fully endorsed by the Seventh Special Session.[19]

UNIDO, which has so far functioned as a small operational program of the General Assembly, is to become a specialized agency following a conference of plenipotentiaries to be convened by the Secretary-General in Vienna at the end of 1976. Through its enlarged set-up, UNIDO will provide a forum for consultations between the developed and developing countries, and negotiation of agreements in the field of industry. The new fund, working in conjunction with UNIDO, will encourage and support industrial development projects, paying special attention to the needs of the least developed, the landlocked, and islands.

The industrialized countries have not shown any particular enthusiasm for the conversion of UNIDO into a specialized agency, believing that this would require extra voluntary contributions from them for UNIDO and the fund. This, however, will not prevent UNIDO from emerging as a specialized agency by 1977.

The Seventh Special Session also endorsed the proposal for the establishment of an industrial technological bank, which would promote a greater flow to developing countries of information permitting the selection of appropriate technologies, in particular advanced technologies. A complementary proposal relates to the establishment of an international center for the exchange of technological information, which would enable developing countries to share research findings relevant to their needs.[20]

Kissinger's proposal for an International Energy Institute, which would assist developing countries in energy resources research and development, is also under study in the UN.

Kissinger's latest proposal for an Industrial Resources Bank (IRB), which he presented at UNCTAD IV, is designed to stimulate private investment in the development of mineral resources, including oil and natural gas, in developing countries.[21] The bank, which would raise funds through the issue of commodity bonds, "would promote more rational, systematic and equitable development of resources in developing nations." The proposal was rejected by UNCTAD IV by a 33–31 vote, but the United States intends to pursue it further, and has submitted it for consideration at the Paris talks.[22]

NOTES

1. *Declaration and Plan of Action on Industrial Development and Cooperation,* drawn up by the Second Ministerial Meeting of the Group of 77, Algiers, February 15, 1975, UN Doc. E/AC.62/4.

2. UN Doc. A/10112, June 13, 1975.

3. See Francisco Casanova Alvarez, La Carta o la Guerra, Organizacion Editorial Novaro (Mexico: 1975), pp.147–74.

4. United Nations, General Assembly, *Resolution 3281* (XXIX), December 12, 1974.

5. Figures quoted from IBRD, *Capital Requirements of Developing Countries: 1975–1980,* DC/75–10.

6. United Nations, *World Plan of Action on Science and Technology,* April 18, 1971.

7. United Nations, General Assembly, *Resolution 3362* (S-VII), Section III, September 19, 1975.

8. *1975 Review: Development Cooperation,* OECD (Paris: November 1975), p.23.

9. Figures quoted from *Development Forum,* UNCTAD IV Supplement, March–April 1976, page II.

10. United Nations, *World Economic Survey, 1974,* E/5665.

11. United Nations, General Assembly, *Resolution 3202* (S-VI), Section IV, May 16, 1974.

12. UNCTAD Resolution TAD/RES/89(IV), May 30, 1976.

13. UNCTAD Resolution TAD/RES/88(IV), May 30, 1976.

14. U.S. Mission to the United Nations, Press release, May 6, 1976.

15. United Nations, General Assembly, *Resolution 3202* (S-VI), Section V, May 16, 1974.

16. New York *Times,* May 27, 1976; *The Economist,* June 26, 1976.

17. Simon Albert Gonsalvi, "The Latin American Economic System: Turning Point for Regional Economic Integration," *Venezuela Now,* March 15, 1976, p.72.

18. UN Doc. D/10112, Chapter IV.

19. United Nations, General Assembly, *Resolution 3362* (S-VII), Section IV, September 19, 1975.

20. United Nations, General Assembly, *Resolution 3362* (S-VII), Section III, September 19, 1975.

21. U.S. Mission to the United Nations, Press release, May 6, 1976.

22. New York *Times,* June 19, 1976.

The institutional response to the movement toward a new international order can be placed in three categories. First, there is the effort to reform and rejuvenate the economic and social sectors of the UN system. This is based primarily on the report of the Group of 25 Experts appointed by the 29th General Assembly.[1] Second, new institutions are being created within the UN system to deal with specific needs, for example, the World Food Council and the IFAD. Third, new forums and groups are being established outside the UN system.

REPORT OF THE GROUP OF 25

The report of the Group of 25 Experts is the most comprehensive effort in recent years to deal with the intricacies and complexities of the UN system and to propose extensive reforms in order to make the system respond to new challenges. The Ad Hoc Committee on the Restructuring of the Economic and Social Sectors of the UN system, which was appointed by the 30th General Assembly, has agreed to use all available documentation in the course of its work, but as its records show,[2] the report of the Group of Experts is constantly referred to by various delegations as the major document. It will be therefore useful to examine the recommendations of the group, in some detail.

The group, which had Al Noor Kassum of Tanzania as its chairman and Richard N. Gardner of the United States as its general rapporteur, took as its mandate the General Assembly request which called for " a study containing proposals on structural changes within the UN system so as to make it fully capable of dealing with problems of international economic cooperation in a comprehensive manner."[3] The committee identified nine problem areas—fragmentation of effort, insufficient emphasis on the search for consensus, absence of small negotiating groups which could privately thrash out complex issues, lack of high-level representation at many UN meetings, artificial separation of planning and operations, concern about the quality of staff, functions not yet adequately performed in the institutional structure, less than universal participation in some of the international economic institutions, and problems relating to decentralization. While the committee was not able to deal with many of these problem areas in a substantive manner, it came up with several specific proposals for restructuring; and a recommendation to appropriate UN groups for further study of those issues it was not able to give much attention to.

The main proposals of the group relate to the strengthening of the role of the General Assembly and the Economic and Social Council, consolidation of the operational structures for development, and establishment of a close link between policy and operations, and improvements in the Secretariat support facilities.

The group would like to see the UN practice of convening ad hoc global conferences abandoned; instead, the General Assembly would convene special sessions, along the lines of the Sixth and the Seventh Special Sessions, whenever necessary. This would enable the General Assembly to focus and act directly on urgent problems of global concern. The proposal seems to have received some support in the Ad Hoc Committee; but it is worth noting that the Conference on the Law of the Seas, which was first convened in 1974 is continuing to hold further sessions; UN conferences on water, and on desertification are planned for 1977; and a Conference on Science and Technology will be held in 1979. If the experts' proposal is adopted, presumably such conferences beyond 1978 and 1979 will be organized in the framework of special sessions; and on subjects like population, environment, and women, where previous conferences have asked for similar conferences to be held every ten years or so, there would be no fixed periodicity for future conferences.

The group argues for the revitalization of the role and functions of the Economic and Social Council.

> If the United Nations System is to contribute effectively to the solution of international economic problems, there must be a central organ within the system where the inputs from the various United Nations bodies can be shaped into coherent policies for development and international economic cooperation, and where there can be a central review of the mutual consistency of actions taken sectorally, particularly the interdependence of decisions on trade, monetary reform and development financing and of decisions taken in the fields of agriculture, industrialization and other areas.[4]

To this end, the group recommends that the council organize its program on a biennial basis, with subject-oriented short sessions spread throughout the calendar year (except during the General Assembly period). Except for regional economic commissions and the commissions dealing with statistics, narcotic drugs, development planning, transnational corporations, and human rights, the existing subsidiary bodies of the council would be abolished and the council would take over direct responsibility for their work. Member states would be asked to ensure high level representation, relevant to the subject matter to be discussed at a given session.

One of the major innovations in the functioning of the council would be "the establishment by the Council of small negotiating groups (with 10–30 members) to deal with key economic issues identified by it as requiring further negotiations with a view to bringing about agreed solutions."[5] The idea is to permit serious negotiations to take place, without public posturing and recriminations. Such negotiating groups have already been used by other institutions such as IMF and UNCTAD. The Group of Experts feels that the work done by the negotiating groups, which would be serviced by appropriate secretariat organs including UNCTAD, would greatly enhance the effectiveness of the final positions adopted by the council.

The proposal for negotiating groups has been formulated in the light of the complaints from the industrialized countries that the council resolutions on economic issues in the past have been very often one-sided, and have paid scant attention to the need to synthesize and harmonize differing views. The Group of Experts suggests the creation of negotiating groups on an experimental basis. It further suggests that in its first biennial period, the council should not establish negotiating groups to deal with subjects already under consideration in UNCTAD. At the end of this initial period, there should be a review to determine what further progress is warranted. If such groups were to function effectively, the need for establishment of negotiating groups outside the UN system (such as those created as a follow-up to the Paris Conference on International Economic Cooperation) may diminish, and eventually disappear.

As for Secretariat support facilities, the Group of Experts stresses the need to consolidate and coordinate policy and operational structures, in recognition of the interdependence of economic issues. The group was not dealing with the autonomous specialized agencies, and did not make recommendations on their structures and functions. It does propose an Advisory Committee on Economic Cooperation and Development, which would include, apart from the heads of the UN regional economic commissions, the heads of IMF, the World Bank, UNCTAD, UNIDO, ILO, FAO, the UN Educational, Scientific, and Cultural Organization, and the World Health Organization (WHO). The Committee, as an interagency mechanism, would review the world economic and social situation, and bring those issues that require international action to the attention of the Economic and Social Council.

The reorganization of the economic and social sectors of the UN system would require, in the opinion of the group, the establishment of a new post of Director General for Development and International Economic Cooperation directly under the UN secretary general. The director general, who would normally come from a developing country, would be assisted (as Figure 2 shows) by two deputy directors general, one for research and policy, and the other for operations. The research and policy sector would take up the present functions of the UN Department of Economic and Social Affairs, while the operational sector would be organized as the new UN Development Authority (UNDA) through a consolidation of the existing development units such as UNDP, UNFPA, UNEP, WFP, the Special Fund, and other smaller funds. The United Nations International Children's Emergency Fund (UNICEF), because of its special character, has been excluded from this list. The proposed structure would ensure a continuing link between research and policy staff and operational staff, and by bringing all the development funds together, increase the effectiveness of the UN's work on development. The Group of Experts feels that the proposed reorganization could be carried out without any increase in staffing costs; if anything, this could result in considerable savings that could be channeled to the operational programs.

The Group of Experts draws attention to the need for closer relationship between the UN development agencies and the World Bank group.

> The value of the UN development work in the past has been reduced because of a somewhat inadequate working relationship between the United Nations and the International Bank for Reconstruction and Development. There has been a danger in the United Nations undertaking, on a smaller scale, with more limited resources, some of the same functions as the Bank. The risk of duplication and overlapping has occurred, especially in the preparation of country programmes and in visits of a succession of missions to discuss development plans. It has also occurred with regard to assistance activities in the field of development planning.[6]

The group advocates a close working relationship between the new UNDA and the World Bank, coordination and harmonization of the country programs of UNDA and the World Bank, and fullest possible exchange of information, experience, ideas, and personnel between the two entities.

The discussions that have taken place in the Ad Hoc Committee on Restructuring show general support for the interlinking of policy and operational structures and for the coordination of the UN's development effort.

The heads of the specialized agencies who spoke before the committee defended the records of their own organizations and cautioned against "over-coordination." While most delegations were offering only tentative ideas, it was evident that they had special interests and concerns relating to various

FIGURE 2
New United Nations Secretariat Structure for Global Economic Cooperation

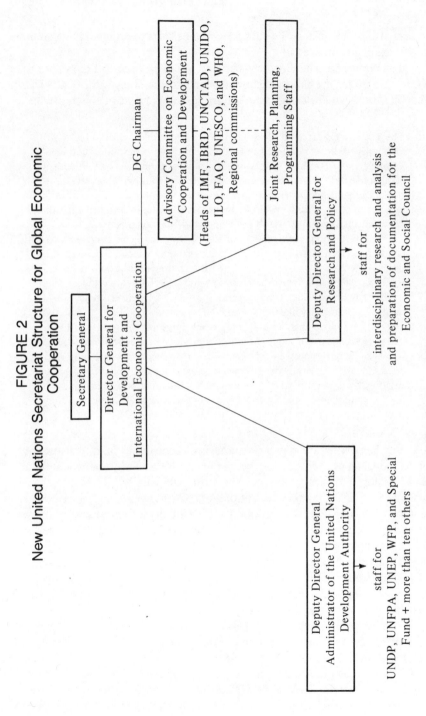

Source: *A New United Nations Structure for Global Economic Cooperation.*

sectors of UN activities and would be wary of efforts to bring all kinds of units under one giant umbrella.

The views of a group including several senior government representatives which met under the chairmanship of the deputy administrator of UNDP, I. G. Patel, in New York in May 1976 are quite pertinent in this regard:

> The group considered the feasibility of a merger of all operational funds. Generally, there was acceptance that while a single operational fund which administered a carefully-tailored set of programs is perhaps conceptually an ideal solution, it may not represent an optimum solution when several important practical considerations are also taken into account. The process by which the several funds would be merged into a single entity might entail potential disadvantages which might preclude any such action.
>
> For one thing, governments might be less willing to contribute to a single fund rather than to a multiplicity of funds which recognized their special interests. It was felt that while earmarking contributions or making funds available on a "trust fund" basis could overcome this problem, there could be political difficulties in operating under one central agency a truly multipurpose activity like that of the UNDP and several other "earmarked" activities which in their totality may reach large proportions. Further, to merge the funds into a single entity might produce a monolithic bureaucracy increasingly unresponsive to the needs of governments of developing countries. However, generally the group also felt that the consolidation of certain existing funds, permitting the maintenance of their identity, and an openness to accommodate future funds within a consolidated framework offered promise and should be actively pursued.[7]

Further discussion of the restructuring problem needs to focus not only on the mechanics, but also on the changing objectives in the economic and social sector. The UN system has shown its adaptability, in recent years, to new needs by creating new institutions—UNFPA for population, UNEP for environment, and IFAD for agricultural development. But, it has shown much less willingness to look at the existing structures to find out if they are still relevant. The report of the Group of Experts also suffers from this shortcoming. It suggests the abolition of a few of the subsidiary bodies of the Economic and Social Council. But it does not try to evaluate separately the performance of various operational units and does not fully deal with the question of what their revised objectives should be.

The concept of technical cooperation is undergoing major changes at the present. The need for international experts is diminishing, the developing countries want direct control over international programs in their territories, and they want as much untied aid as possible. These questions should be very carefully looked into before the UN decides to consolidate and renovate its economic and social program. The case of UNDP, the major arm of UN development assistance, highlights all of these problems.

MULTILATERAL ASSISTANCE

UNDP has served as the main instrument for providing multilateral technical assistance to developing countries. UNDP was set up in 1965 through a merger of two of the UN's earlier technical assistance programs— the Expanded Programme of Technical Assistance and the United Nations Special Fund. UNDP's main program areas are: survey and assessment of development assets and potentials; stimulation of capital investments; training, adaptation, and application of modern technologies to local conditions; and economic and social planning.

A recent summary of UNDP activities indicates that UNDP provides to developing countries each year 10,000 international experts, 5,000 fellowships for study abroad, about $47 million worth of equipment and about $35 million worth of specialized technical services.[8] UNDP is also authorized now to provide limited amounts of capital for construction of pilot production facilities in industry and agriculture. The annual program expenditure by UNDP is around $315 million a year. Though this constitutes four-fifths of the UN outlay for development assistance, it represents less than 3 percent of the total official aid. It is estimated that the industrialized countries belonging to OECD provide nearly $11 billion in aid each year, while nongovernmental organizations are responsible for providing approximately $1.3 billion every year.

A second major source of multilateral technical assistance in the UN system is UNFPA. UNFPA now provides $90 million in assistance to developing countries annually, for projects ranging from family planning to data collection, research, training, education, and communications in the population field.

The WFP, which operates as a joint undertaking of the United Nations and FAO, provides food aid to developing countries in order to help them in carrying out development projects. It also seeks to meet emergency food needs. For the 1975–76 biennial, the program received pledges of $600 million in support of its operations.

UNICEF, a well-known program of the United Nations, has operated for many years a world-wide technical assistance program in the areas of maternal and child health, training and education, and family planning. UNICEF's annual program budget, which runs to about $100 million, is expected to go up to $200 million in the next few years.

Other smaller funds and programs in the UN system which provde technical assistance are the Capital Development Fund, the Revolving Fund for Natural Resources, the Environment Fund, and so on. The UN has also coordinated emergency aid and assistance to deal with specific situations from time to time. The Special Fund, which was established in 1974 to provide emergency aid to the developing countries affected by the sharp increase in oil prices, was one such operation.

Toward the end of 1975 UNDP was faced with a financial crisis, as a result of overcommitment on projects, shortfalls in anticipated contributions, impact of inflation on its administrative and program costs, and managerial problems. The administration of UNDP changed around the same time, and the new administrator, Bradford Morse, has undertaken vigorous efforts to resolve UNDP's financial crisis.

The financial crisis in UNDP, as well as shortfalls in anticipated contributions for many other multilateral assistance programs, has brought to the fore the whole question of the future of multilateral technical assistance. When UNDP was established in 1965, the UN was expected to provide mainly technical experts, equipment, and services within the framework of its development assistance program, most of these coming from the industrialized countries. The situation is different today, in that many of the developing countries can find local experts or experts from neighboring countries. They remain short of capital and, in some cases, equipment. In response to the continuing need for training, an extensive network of national and regional institutions has already been established. The demand for international experts is thus going to go down rather rapidly.

UNDP switched some time ago to country programming; and the way this works now, there is a diminishing need for UNDP managerial and administrative staff to devote full-time, on-the-spot, attention to country programs. Many of the recipient governments determine their own priorities and goals, using very little external advice. Such advice as is needed could be provided through periodic visits to the countries concerned by senior officials and experts. The number and staffing of field offices could then be reduced and rationalized.

One of the reasons why the delivery of multilateral assistance is so costly is the use of international organizations as executing agents of assistance programs. The executing agents charge their own percentage for administrative and infrastructure costs ranging from 14 to 21 percent. If one were to add the infrastructure costs incurred by the donor agency, the executing agency, and finally the recipient agency, the amount left for actual technical assistance comes down to a very small percentage of the total. What the countries are asking for now is direct delivery of multilateral assistance to them as far as possible; they would like to choose outside experts or executing agencies themselves, and only in cases where absolutely necessary. Direct implementation by governments may reduce costs and increase the effectiveness of programs.

DEVELOPMENT ASSISTANCE IN THE FUTURE

The future of multilateral assistance seems therefore to be tied to delivery of as much aid as possible directly to countries, use of international experts only when absolutely necessary, reduction in administrative and infrastructure costs, and assistance in development planning, in accordance with the countries' own requirements and needs. For many developing countries, multilateral assistance is still preferable to bilateral assistance, for political and practical reasons. They prefer not to receive bilateral aid directly from some countries, and they would rather deal with multilateral agencies, as they are likely to attach fewer strings to their assistance. It is therefore likely that there will be a continuing demand for multilateral assistance, but only if its concept, role, and structure are revised radically, along the lines mentioned above. The new UNDA and all the funds under UN management will have to function in this new context.

As the resources for development assistance available through the UN system are unlikely to expand at a rapid rate, the UN will have to establish priorities so that its resources can be put to the most effective and efficient use. Assistance to the least developed countries (LDCs) is obviously a high priority.* Assistance to the non-oil-producing countries, which have been most seriously affected by the increase in oil prices and by general inflationary pressures, (the MSAs) is another priority.† Many of the countries included in the two lists are, in fact, the same. The World Bank has produced the list of a somewhat larger group of countries, with less than $200 per capita income in 1973.‡ None of these categories needs to be considered the sole criterion for providing assistance. But there is a clear argument for assisting the broad group of the poorest countries: (1) because their people live in conditions of

---

*The list of the least-developed countries (LDCs) was established by the UN General Assembly Resolution 2768 (XXVI) of November 18, 1971. It includes: Afghanistan, Bhutan, Botswana, Burundi, Chad, Dahomey, Ethiopia, Guinea, Haiti, Laos, Lesotho, Malawi, Maldives, Mali, Nepal, Niger, Rwanda, Sikkim, Somalia, Sudan, Uganda, Tanzania, Upper Volta, Western Samoa, and Yemen. Four other countries were added to this list through the resolution of the Economic and Social Council 1976 (LIX) of July 30, 1975: Bangladesh, Central African Republic, Democratic Yemen, and Gambia.

†The list of MSAs established by the UN Secretary General comprises 42 countries. The original list included Bangladesh, Cameroon, Central African Republic, Chad, Dahomey, El Salvador, Ethiopia, Ghana, Guinea, Guyana, Haiti, Honduras, India, Ivory Coast, Kenya, Khmer Republic, Laos, Lesotho, Malagasy Republic, Mali, Mauritania, Niger, Pakistan, Rwanda, Senegal, Sierra Leone, Somalia, Sri Lanka, Sudan, Tanzania, Upper Volta, Yemen Arab Republic, and Democratic Yemen. Another nine countries were added to the list later: Afghanistan, Burma, Burundi, Cape Verde Islands, Egypt, Guinea-Bissau, Mozambique, Uganda, and Western Samoa.

‡The World Bank Atlas 1975 lists countries with less than $200 per capita as follows: Afghanistan, Bangladesh, Benin (People's Republic of), Bhutan, Burma, Burundi, Cambodia, Central African Republic, Chad, Comoro Islands, Ethiopia, Gambia (The), Guinea, Haiti, India, Indonesia, Kenya, Laos, Lesotho, Malagasy Republic, Malawi, Maldive Islands, Mali, Nepal, Niger, Pakistan, Portuguese Timor, Rwanda, Sierra Leone, Sikkim, Somalia, South Vietnam, Sri Lanka, Sudan, Tanzania, Togo, Uganda, Upper Volta, Vietnam (Democratic Republic of), Yemen Arab Republic, Yemen (People's Democratic Republic of), Zaire.

extreme poverty and misery and (2) because they face far greater obstacles than other developing countries in moving toward goals of economic and social justice.

Special emphasis will have to be placed on rural development, as most of the poor in the developing countries live in the rural areas. In addition to agricultural development, continuing attention needs to be paid to the provision of basic facilities relating to credit, marketing, transport, roads, water supply, elementary education, and health requirements. Though everybody talks of "integrated rural development," it is important to recognize that there are no standard models for rural development, and that projects have to be tailored to the specific needs and requirements of each given area or region.

Varying criteria may have to be evolved for different types of programs. UNFPA, for example, is planning to establish its own priorities for resource allocation based on a combination of factors relating to total population, per capita national income, rate of population growth, and levels of fertility, infant mortality, and population density.[9]

PERSONNEL

Personnel policies and practices in international institutions are of direct relevance to the revised objectives these institutions are setting for themselves. To this end, the Group of Experts offers several proposals: competitive examinations for UN service, a program of "prerecruitment training" to assist developing countries in the training of candidates for posts subject to geographical distribution, increase in the proportion of women in the professional category, and establishment of a UN Fellows Programme to bring to the system young people of superior quality from all over the world. The group suggests that the UN agencies should move toward a unified personnel system, including a unified system of salaries, grading, conditions of service, and recruitment, and proposes that the International Civil Service Commission (which is already operational) be given additional powers and responsibilities for this purpose.[10]

There is a residual personnel problem in all the UN institutions, in varying degrees, which defies easy solution. Because of the formal or informal quota system, which is primarily based on contributions, and also because technical expertise was largely concentrated in the rich world in the early postwar years, a very large number of professional jobs were given to European and American nationals, many of whom by the influx of time have now moved up to very senior positions. The political complexion of these organizations has changed, with the emergence of the Third World majorities, but the responsibility for implementing decisions still rests with the senior officials, most of whom come from the Western world.

Dr. Kenneth King, former minister of economic development in Guyana, and currently an assistant director general in FAO, provides the following personal view of this situation:

> Some staff members often lack experience in developing countries, are often ignorant of the developmental process as applied to unindustrialized countries, often display an absence of commitment to development, are sometimes arrogant and are sometimes so obsessed with what they consider to be the superiority of their "industrial culture" that they find it difficult to devise policies, programmes and projects which consciously take into account the cultures of the people whom they are supposed to serve, and the stage of economic evolution of the country they are advising.[11]

Tensions are bound to arise, as the pressure for changes in the Secretariat rises and as new donors and other developing countries seek opportunities for their own nominees at senior policy-making and coordinating levels. The top level of the UN bureaucracy will have to change, but how this can be achieved remains an open question. Dr. King suggests, among other things, a drastic reduction in the contributions of the United States and other industrialized countries, and thus, by implication, a reduction in their representation in the Secretariat and other agencies.

While some deliberate adjustments at the top level will have to be made in order to provide greater representation to the Third World and women, the composition of the international civil service can be improved, in time, by carrying out the recommendations of the Group of 25.

PROLIFERATION OF INTERNATIONAL ORGANIZATIONS

Students of international institutions notice a curious phenomenon today. While there is an increasing insistence on coordination and streamlining of operations, international organizations continue to proliferate. In the field of population, UNFPA was established as the operational arm of the UN, to complement the research and policy-making functions of the population division. In the field of environment, a new institution—the UNEP—was created following the Stockholm Conference on Environment in 1972. In the field of food and agriculture, there were only two institutions for many years—FAO and WFP. Now we have the World Food Council and IFAD. UNIDO, for many years a program of the General Assembly, is now becoming a specialized agency. UNDP is managing several new, small funds, such as the Capital Development Fund and the Revolving Fund for Natural Resources. The UN

Conference on Human Settlements (Vancouver, June 1976) has proposed the consolidation of all the UN units dealing with human settlements into a new structure.

A NEW TRADE AGENCY

The report of the Group of Experts refers to the possibility of establishing an international trade organization which in effect would incorporate UNCTAD and GATT into a single organization with two chapters, one concerned with broad policy and the other with trade negotiations, both using a common secretariat.[12] In the short run, the group would like GATT to be brought into formal relationship with the UN; UNCTAD is already a part of the UN system.

It may be recalled that soon after World War II, there was an effort on the part of the United States to promote the establishment of a UN-related International Trade Organization (ITO). A charter for ITO was adopted at the International Conference on Trade and Employment held in Havana in November 1948, and an interim commission for ITO set up. The charter emphasized the free interplay of economic forces in international trade, and thus reflected mainly the trade philosophy of the Western industrialized countries.

The charter never came into force, as the United States, which had taken such a leading part in formulating the proposals for ITO, eventually did not find it possible to accept the charter. The business community in the United States felt that the charter did not go far enough in the removal of trade barriers on the part of foreign countries, the escape clauses were too numerous, and the charter contemplated too much regulation by states, to the detriment of private enterprise.[13] Though the plans for an international trade agency were thus frustrated, many of the policies formulated in the ITO Charter were later put into operation through GATT.

The proposals for a new ITO have some similarities with the Havana Charter, but it would now be based on the experience acquired by two existing institutions, GATT and UNCTAD. It has been suggested that an ITO could also deal with related issues—transfer of technology, transnational corporations, restrictive business practices, and investments.[14]

An immediate attempt toward the establishment of an ITO seems unlikely, but the proposals for the new organization will remain under study and consideration, and may come up for further discussion, depending on future developments, within UNCTAD and GATT.

In addition to the new institutions within the UN framework, the number of regional or specialized banks and funds to provide development capital or aid continues to grow. Kuwait has set up its own development fund; so have the Arab countries as a group; and now OPEC has decided to establish a $1 billion fund to aid poor countries.

U.S. Secretary of State Kissinger has proposed the establishment of several new institutions in each one of his major international speeches, the latest being the International Resources Bank, which would promote private investment in the developing countries. He also constantly talks about the need for an International Energy Institute, which would help developing countries solve their energy problem.

MAJOR TRENDS

Though this proliferation of international organizations seems confusing, there are several major trends that can be discerned at this time:

1. It seems clear that the number of funds and programs dealing with investment and aid will continue to grow. Some of these, such as IFAD, are being established to meet specific needs. Others are being established at the behest of groups of donor countries, OPEC, for example. These funds or programs, some of which may be associated with existing institutions, are expected to be run by small, specialist staffs, with flexible mandates.

2. A related development is the establishment or expansion of regional institutions for Asia, Africa, West Asia, and Latin America. In some of the larger geographical regions, subregional groupings are coming into their own. For instance, the Caribbean countries, apart from participating in Latin American instititions, are in the process of creating specialized organizations for their own area.

3. As the need for international technical assistance and for international experts diminishes, the role of older international institutions active in these areas is also likely to diminish. All of them may have to reduce their field offices, their staff, and their administrative costs.

In fact, it may be necessary now to consider a rationalization and realignment of the structures and jurisdictions of these intergovernmental agencies, so as to fit them in a new scheme of global priorities. At a conference organized by the Stanley Foundation in Baden Bei Wien (Austria) in June 1975, several participants suggested that "this problem can best be approached by an international conference of plenipotentiaries with the aim of achieving rationalization between the intergovernmental bodies and agencies as well as a better and more efficient relationship between them and the United Nations."[15]

4. Some of the jobs now being performed by international experts could be performed in the future at much lower costs by consulting firms. Most of these consulting firms are now based in the West; but given proper encourage-

ment and opportunity, many such groups, with adequate technical capability, could emerge in countries like India, Pakistan, and Mexico.

5. There will be a continuing role for the UN agencies and institutions in such fields as population, children's welfare, refugees, food and agriculture, environment, and industrialization. Programs such as UNFPA, UNICEF and the UN Office of the High Commissioner for Refugees (UNHCR), which have a proven record in delivering assistance, may be asked to expand their services and programs further. New institutions like UNIDO and IFAD will acquire increasing importance as they become operational. If the Law of the Sea Conference comes to a successful conclusion, the UN may be given some follow-up responsibilities through the International Seabed Authority.

6. Interchangeability of staff among international organizations may become an important factor in increasing their effectiveness. Staff members in the UN system can move from one organization to another fairly easily in theory; but lack of job security and loss of promotion opportunity keep most of them working within their organizations. Greater mobility for the brightest and the best will tend to bring them to those areas of UN concern which are among the most urgent and the most challenging at any given time. The establishment of a unified system for the entire UN system, as suggested by the Group of 25 Experts, will go a long way toward meeting this need.

There are many structural and functional changes and innovations now under way or being contemplated. Hopefully they will lead all those specialized agencies and organs of the United Nations which are involved in supporting national programs to revise and adjust their program objectives and targets in such a way that they would respond directly to the minimum needs of the people in the developing countries. The organizations involved in developmental assistance (for example, the World Bank, UNDP and UNFPA) are moving in this direction at varying paces. ILO plans now to support national action programs developed in the context of the basic needs approach adopted by the World Employment Conference. WHO and UNICEF are committed on the basis of a joint study commissioned in 1973 to supporting primary health care programs which would rely heavily on community-level workers and a simplified health technology. Other organizations also may follow suit, in the years to come.

The definition of minimum needs and the setting of program targets will have to be undertaken by each country in the context of its own traditions, practices, and requirements. International organizations can, however, help by spurring community-based action, providing new knowledge and technology where relevant, and encouraging innovative projects and approaches. The future effectiveness of these organizations will depend on how swiftly they can put into practice new approaches they all accept in principle.

NOTES

1. *A New United Nations Structure for Global Economic Cooperation,* UN Sales No. E 75. 11.A. 7, 1975.

2. Addendum to the Report of the Ad Hoc Committee on the Restructuring of the Economic and Social Sectors of the UN System, GA *Official Records,* 31st session, Supp. 34A (A/31/34/Add. 11), 1976.

3. Report of the Ad Hoc Committee on Restructuring of the Economic and Social Sectors of the UN System, GA, *Official Records,* 30th Session: Supplement 5 (A 10005), 1975.

4. *A New UN Structure,* op. cit., p. 13.

5. Ibid., p. 15.

6. Ibid., p. 46.

7. *Report of the Seventh Annual Conference on UN Procedures* (Muscatine, Iowa: Stanley Foundation, 1976), pp. 18–19.

8. *The UN Development Programme: Questions and Answers,* UNDP, New York, September 1975, p. 3.

9. See UNDP Governing Council Doc. DP/186, May 4, 1976.

10. *A New UN Structure,* op. cit., pp. 27–29.

11. Dr. Kenneth King, "Boomerang Aid," *The New Internationalist,* October 1975, p. 21.

12. *A New UN Structure,* op. cit., pp. 54–55.

13. See V.A. Seyid Muhammad, *The Legal Framework of World Trade* (London: Stevens and Sons Ltd., 1958), p. 21.

14. *A New UN Structure,* op. cit., Annex II, p. 74.

15. *Coordination of the Economic and Social Activities of the United Nations* (Muscatine, Iowa: Stanley Foundation, 1975), p. 13.

8

A NEW INTERNATIONAL
ECONOMIC ORDER

The third quarter of the twentieth century saw more than 90 countries emerge into political independence. The next quarter-century is likely to witness an accelerating movement in pursuit of economic freedom. The vision of a new international economic order, flawed as it is, will gain an increasing number of adherents; and it is not so much the problems of war and peace, but the problems of economic and social development, that will become the focal points of international relations.

The Seventh Special Session did not exactly start this era. Development issues had been debated in international forums for more than 20 years; and we were well into the second UN Development Decade when the Seventh Special Session took place. But the session should be considered the point in time when the political will of the developing countries to seek changes in the international economic order merged with the emerging realities of interdependence to start a new era in political and economic relations.

The process of negotiations and bargaining needed to bring about changes at the international level is going to be complex and tortuous. The Group of 77 will have to retain its unity; and given differing economic, social, and cultural backgrounds among the members, this is not going to be easy. On the other side, many of the industrialized countries will be loath to give up even a part of the economic power they have wielded so long.

The North-South dialogue at the international level needs to be complemented by vigorous national efforts to alleviate poverty. Changes in the internal economic order, which will help to raise agricultural and industrial production and to reduce the gap between the rich and the poor within developing countries, will be in many ways even more difficult to achieve than changes in the international order. But in reality there are no alternatives to pursuing such changes.

REASON FOR OPTIMISM

How does the future look at this time? In three interrelated areas, there are definite reasons for optimism.

Food

Food production is the first. Though North America will have to continue exporting food in large quantities, food production in developing countries can be increased and improved in the next 25 years. Self-sufficiency may not be attained by many countries, and is indeed not a practical proposition for many of them. But those countries which have already benefited from the Green Revolution can and should be able to increase their production and to improve their internal distribution arrangements. A rational, worldwide system of food security and distribution which can ensure that nobody goes hungry is within our reach now, while enabling food-exporting countries to make a decent profit on their exports or to work out suitable barter arrangements for products they need.

Population

Population growth remains an area of critical concern; but there are definite signs that the rate of growth is slowing down, and may slow down further by 1985. Even then there may be 1.5 to 2.25 billion extra people in the year 2000,* and most of them will be born in the Third World. Adequate nutrition, shelter, housing, health care, and education will be needed for them, as it is for the 2 billion poor in the world today. These needs can be taken care of only through comprehensive development planning which ensures simultaneous, interrelated growth in all sectors.

Industrial Growth

Industrial growth in the developing countries is going to pick up. Whether 25 percent of the world's industry will be located in the developing world in

---

*The lower estimate comes from AID's Office of Population; 2.25 billion is the medium variant projection provided by the UN.

the year 2000 (a goal set by the Group of 77) remains a matter of conjecture. But almost certainly the Third World will have a much larger industrial sector than it has today. It is to be hoped that in planning and implementing their industrial strategy, developing countries will keep a clear perspective of their needs in the agricultural and the industrial sectors, and will concentrate on labor-intensive industries which will generate employment for their people.

More development capital and aid is likely to become available through the World Bank Group and through some of the institutions being set up by OPEC countries individually or collectively. Official development assistance may also grow, at least in the case of the Scandinavian countries, the United Kingdom, and the Netherlands; but whether it will reach the 0.7 percent target in all the industrialized countries remains to be seen. The needs of the poorest countries are likely to receive greater attention, partly because of humanitarian considerations and partly because they do not need a massive volume of assistance. The World Bank puts it at an extra $2.5–3.5 billion over and above what is being provided yearly now.[1]

Private foreign investment in many developing countries may continue to grow, despite continuing controversy on its role. Very often both the capital and the technology that may be needed in these countries are available through the same transnational corporations or consortia. India, for instance, which was wary of foreign investment for many years, is now allowing transnationals to come into some selected areas, with appropriate guarantees and provisos. It is also necessary to remember that in the United States, as well as most other industrialized countries, both capital and technology are generally in private hands, and it is illogical to expect that in international forums these countries will adopt a posture which is contrary to these private interests. Under pressure, they may, however, agree to greater regulation and control of the activities of the transnational corporations.

PROBLEM AREAS

The sticky areas are commodity trade, access to industrialized countries' markets, repayment of debts, and further reforms in the international monetary and financial systems. Indexation for commodity prices is unlikely to be accepted by the industrialized countries; but compensatory financing schemes may be enlarged. Multilateral commodity arrangements will be pursued by UNCTAD and by the developing countries involved in the Paris talks, but the United States does not seem well-disposed toward accepting such broad arrangements.* Some agreement on funding and maintenance of buffer stocks may not, however, be so difficult to achieve.

Export of manufactures and semimanufactures from developing countries to industrialized countries may expand through extension of the GSP. If the current recession in the industrialized countries gives way to economic recovery—and there are signs that this is already happening—the industrialized countries may agree to provide to the developing countries easier access to their markets.

The problem of debts will be the subject of many international negotiations. The Group of 77 has called for cancellation of debts of LDCs and rescheduling of commercial debts over a period of at least 25 years. It has also proposed a debtor-creditor conference to establish overall guidelines for negotiation of debts. Creditor countries, however, take the position that action to ease the debt burden should be undertaken on a case-by-case basis. Through further negotiations, the poorest countries may eventually get a debt moratorium, while the debts of many other developing countries may be rescheduled, and, in some cases, repayment conditions made easier.

Further reforms in the international monetary and financial arrangements will require increased participation of developing countries (particularly OPEC countries) in the IMF and the World Bank Group. While the operations of these groups will continue to expand, given the belief of many industrialized countries that these institutions are best suited to handle the extra demand for development capital, other institutions—international and regional—are likely to emerge, through the cooperative efforts of OPEC members and other developing countries.

The process of future international negotiations on international economic issues will be increasingly conditioned by the nature of the internal economies of the developing and the industrialized countries. The unity of the Third World is today based on political as well as economic factors. Anticolonialism is the political factor, and poverty, of varying degrees, the economic one. Anticolonialism will probably survive until the next generation, and in that it affects the attitudes of both the elite and the masses in the developing countries, it will continue to provide a rallying point for both the groups. But poverty does not affect all the strata of a developing society in the

---

*A joint statement issued by Secretary of Treasury Simon and Secretary of State Kissinger on June 1, 1976, in Washington indicated that the US was prepared to participate in preparatory talks but only "on a case-by-case examination of arrangements to improve the functioning of the international commodity markets."

same way. While poverty is a daily reality for the masses, for the elite—administrators, entrepreneurs, and other members of the upper classes—it is an intellectual concern. The GNP and per capita figures can be used convincingly to prove that the developing countries are being treated badly, and need a more equitable share of the world's resources. But as greater resources begin to accrue to the developing countries, will their leaders really use them for the benefit of their people?

DIFFERENT PATHS TO DEVELOPMENT

While the leaders of many developing countries genuinely desire to improve the lot of their people, the economic policies they are embarked on now will create divergent paths of development and eventually strain the unity of the Third World in international negotiations. Countries that permit and encourage private enterprise in major sectors of their economies may begin to duplicate the process of growth in some of the industrialized countries, and to that extent will find it easier to deal with those industrialized countries. On the other hand, those that choose to exercise direct state control over major sectors of their economies may find themselves in conflict not only with the industrialized countries, but also with the Third World supporters of private enterprise, when it comes to the question of setting common objectives in international negotiations.

This is a dilemma that developing countries will face to an increasing degree as time goes on. The theme of poverty is unlikely to serve for long as the theme for unity. And if we accept that each country has a right to choose its own path to development, in the light of its own situation, the dilemma cannot be easily resolved. Those who talk of alternative development are right when they point out that each developing country needs to devise its own program to satisfy the minimum needs of its people, without trying to catch up with the rest of the world. But are they also not secretly hoping that all the developing countries will choose the same model of self-reliant economic growth, with distributive social justice? This is where their vision of the future does not seem to focus properly. There will indeed be different paths to development—so different, in fact, that continuing adjustments and negotiations between groups of developing countries will be needed to retain their common front vis-à-vis the industrialized countries. Development of trade, aid, and joint economic ventures among developing countries themselves will be an important factor in maintaining and strengthening this front, and ought to be pursued energetically.

INDUSTRIALIZED COUNTRIES

Internal factors will also condition the positions taken by industrialized countries in negotiations with developing countries. It is, for example, unrealistic to expect that the United States will give up its belief in private foreign investment as the best tool to help the rapid growth of developing countries. For a country whose own economy is based on private enterprise, any other viewpoint will smack of hyprocrisy. The efforts of Secretary Kissinger, which are criticized for not going far enough, must be viewed in this context. This is not to say that the United States cannot do more than what it has done so far. It can and should, indeed, be asked to move farther toward increasing aid, reducing its tariff barriers, regulating the role of transnationals and supporting the transfer of appropriate technology.

Energy-short countries among the members of OECD have in recent years negotiated directly with individual OPEC members to secure their supplies, and should be generally more receptive than the United States to constructive bargaining with OPEC members. Similarly, many European countries, which have long-standing economic ties with Asian, African, and Latin American countries, have shown considerable willingness to pay attention to the demands of the Group of 77 on commodity arrangements and buffer stocks. It was at the insistence of these countries that the United States, the United Kingdom, the Federal Republic of Germany, and Japan finally agreed to join the somewhat vague and general consensus at UNCTAD IV. On their own part, these countries, along with Canada, welcomed the UNCTAD resolution on an integrated commodity program for the prospects it offered for a new and equitable relationship between developed and developing countries.

An equitable distribution of the world's resources will require a reduced growth rate, and a reduction in overconsumption, in the industrialized countries. So far, however, no industrialized country has consciously opted for a lower growth rate. Reduction in consumption, which will eventually have an impact on growth in specific sectors, may however be possible, given effective information campaigns and suitable policy directions. The mass media help to popularize ideas and values rapidly in the industrialized countries. Paul Ehrlich's *Population Bomb* had its greatest impact within the United States; so did Rachel Carson's *Silent Spring.* The Club of Rome's *Limits to Growth* and *Mankind at the Turning Point* created a tremendous impact on the western academic and intellectual circles. Those who argue against overconsumption of resources can and should continue to use mass media in the United States and other industrialized countries to propagate their viewpoint; it may eventually create a deep impact, resulting in major changes in people's habits and customs.

Nongovernmental organizations in the industrialized countries, working in close cooperation with mass media, can play a significant role in promoting an increasing awareness of development issues, by pressuring their governments to take a more open position on the demands of the Third World, and by supporting the case for adjustments and changes needed in growth and consumption patterns. Development groups, which have already emerged in several industrialized countries, show a conscious recognition of their potential impact in these areas.

It is interesting to note that Norway, Sweden, and the Netherlands—the three European countries which have consistently adopted a more open attitude than other industrialized countries on questions of trade, aid, and development—are also the countries where the public opinion as expressed through non-government organizations has been pro-Third World for some time.

ROLE OF SOCIALIST COUNTRIES

The involvement of the East European socialist states in future economic negotiations is unlikely to expand very much. Their trade with selected developing countries will, however, continue to grow, to the extent that these countries are able to provide them with raw materials as well as the manufactures and semimanufactures they need. They will also provide development assistance, on a selective basis.

China stands apart from this group. It has provided assistance for a very small number of carefully selected projects in some developing countries; and this pattern is likely to continue. In the fields of agricultural production, decentralized economic activities, and family planning, China has acquired experience and insights that may prove valuable to other developing countries and that it may be willing to share with them.

ALLEVIATION OF POVERTY

The number of desperately poor people in the developing countries has not diminished significantly despite economic progress achieved by their countries in the last two decades. The gap between the rich and the poor within these countries has not narrowed significantly; in some cases it has even widened. The "trickle down" theory of economic growth which assumes that benefits of development will filter down to reach an ever-increasing number has not worked in practice. The poverty in which people in many developing countries have lived for centuries has now degenerated into a wretchedness and misery that militates against all tolerable norms of human well-being. As E. F. Schumacher says:

Poverty may have been the rule in the past, but misery was not. Poor peasants and artisans have existed from time immemorial; but miserable and destitute villages in their thousands and urban pavement dwellers in their hundreds of thousands—that is a monstrous and scandalous thing which is altogether abnormal in the history of mankind.[2]

As governments of developing countries seek a greater share of the world's resources through international negotiations, they also need to mount an assault on poverty in their own homes, using the extra resources they obtain. As the UN Committee on Development Planning pointed out in 1972:

Governments of many developing countries are aware that their problems are massive, growing and urgent. These problems require urgent attack. Governments who would respond effectively must, in most cases, be prepared to set some radical courses. They must move their poverty-reduction and employment goals from the periphery toward the centre of their development plan. They must become as concerned with income and output generation. They must adopt programmes with direct benefits for the very poor.[3]

The minimum needs that will need to be satisfied, in order to raise the poor out of the circle of poverty, will have to be defined in relation to each country's own situation. In India, for example, the satisfaction of minimum needs has been defined as follows:

A working adult needs 4.5 kg of cereals per week to satisfy minimum energy requirements; in rural areas, other expenditures (on food other than cereals, and on items other than food) represent at least twice the value of cereals, and in urban areas at least three times this value; in an average household, a working adult has to support the equivalent of another adult; a worker requires at least one day of rest each week. This means that the income for a day's work corresponding to the poverty line is equivalent to 3 kg. of cereals in rural areas and 4.5 kg. in urban areas. So as to leave no one below the poverty line, a programme is required that will guarantee work for each rural adult who seeks employment and is able to work and that will also ensure the production of necessary goods.[4]

A national program that provides productive employment will be one of the components of a larger program, including allocation of resources required to generate employment, an efficient system for procurement and distribution of essential goods and services, minimum health care and educational facilities, a policy to take care of housing needs, and nutritional programs for the young and for the mothers.

Further research is needed in most developing countries to establish a definition of minimum needs. Such a definition, once established, will permit the setting of targets and timetables for local, regional, and national efforts. The definition itself obviously will be revised countless times and the standards raised upward as the standard of living rises.

In arguing for fulfillment of minimum needs, we recognize that the definition of these needs and the ordering of priorities will vary from country to country, and that patterns of economic and social development in all the developing countries will not be similar. Future growth may create new problems and new tensions, and continuing research will be needed to anticipate these developments and to propose viable solutions.

But what is clear now is the urgent need for developing countries to reduce the gap between their own rich and poor, as they seek to reduce at the international level the gap between the rich and the poor countries and to obtain a larger share of the earth's resources for their own use. A new international economic order will be meaningless, unless it also helps to bring about a new internal economic order.

THE ROLE OF WOMEN

Social change, as a concomitant to a new internal economic order, should focus on removal of impediments to full participation of various societal sectors in the development effort. In practice, this would require special assistance to minority and disadvantaged groups, to enable them to overcome handicaps in such fields as education and employment.

The role of women is one of the most critical factors in the effort to bring about social change. The emergence of urban women in the Third World in the political and economic life of their countries is a hopeful sign and must be encouraged further. More important, rural women need to be drawn into these activities, and both governmental and extragovernmental efforts will be necessary for this.

In many developing countries, women have traditionally played a major role in the rural economy, participating actively in production, distribution, and marketing. As modernization comes about, there is a tendency to convert women to the middle class, "genteel" values and thus reduce their participation in economically productive sectors. A far-sighted social policy will seek to prevent this diminution in the role of women; on the contrary, it will provide for training and financial support to enable women to play an increasing role in the changing economic life.

Many developing countries (as many developed countries) have not yet fully realized the full potential of women's participation in development; nor have they come to grips with the problem as to how to change traditional male/female role concepts. Yet it is evident that any development effort is bound to remain flawed, unless it seeks to involve fully both men and women.

A NEW ECONOMIC ORDER

The next quarter-century could see the fulfillment of many of the hopes and expectations that have been raised around the world because of the cry for a new international economic order. It is recognized that the present international order and the concomitant national policies cannot be changed overnight. And the changes, when they do come, will differ in their characteristics and impact, from country to country and from region to region. But the outlines of a two-pronged program—aimed at securing an equitable distribution of the world's resources and meeting the minimum needs of the poorest people all over the world—can be clearly seen, and what is needed now is a vigorous pursuit of the policies that will implement this program.

The longest march, as the Chinese say, begins with one tiny step, and that step has already been taken. We need now to keep moving ahead.

The proponents of a new order reject—and rightly so—the concept of charity as the motivating factor behind the changes required. A total emphasis on their right to a fairer share of resources is also not likely to get them very far. A cooperative economic venture—which is joined by both the developed and the developing countries because of their belief in the concept of mutually beneficial interdependence—may be the answer. The international world is full of cynical people who on the basis of long years of experience, tend to distrust anything new unless its value can be clearly demonstrated. Enlightened self-interest could convince even these cynics to become partners in this great venture.

NOTES

1. IBRD, *Capital Requirements of Developing Countries, 1975–1980,* DC/75–10.

2. E. F. Schumacher, in *Voices for Life,* ed. Dom Moraes for UNFPA (New York: Praeger, 1975), p. 135.

3. UN Committee on Development Planning, *Report on the Eighth Session,* E/5447, 1974.

4. *Another Development; The 1975 Dag Hammarskjöld Report on Development and Cooperation* (Uppsala: Dag Hammarskjöld Foundation, 1975), p. 42.

3201 (S-VI). Declaration on the Establishment of a New International Economic Order

The General Assembly

Adopts the following Declaration:

DECLARATION ON THE ESTABLISHMENT OF A NEW INTERNATIONAL ECONOMIC ORDER

We, the Members of the United Nations,

Having convened a special session of the General Assembly to study for the first time the problems of raw materials and development, devoted to the consideration of the most important economic problems facing the world community,

Bearing in mind the spirit, purposes and principles of the Charter of the United Nations to promote the economic advancement and social progress of all peoples,

Solemnly proclaim our united determination to work urgently for THE ESTABLISHMENT OF A NEW INTERNATIONAL ECONOMIC ORDER based on equity, sovereign equality, interdependence, common interest and co-operation among all States, irrespective of their economic and social systems which shall correct inequalities and redress existing injustices, make it possible to eliminate the widening gap between the developed and the developing countries and ensure steadily accelerating economic and social development and peace and justice for present and future generations, and, to that end, declare:

1. The greatest and most significant achievement during the last decades has been the independence from colonial and alien domination of a large number of peoples and nations which has enabled them to become members of the community of free peoples. Technological progress has also been made in all spheres of economic activities in the last three decades, thus providing a solid potential for improving the well-being of all peoples. However, the remaining vestiges of alien and colonial domination, foreign occupation, racial discrimination, *apartheid* and neo-colonialism in all its forms continue to be among the greatest obstacles to the full emancipation and progress of the developing countries and all the peoples involved. The benefits of technological progress are not shared equitably by all members of the international community. The developing countries, which constitute 70 per cent of the world's population, account for only 30 per cent of the world's income. It has proved impossible to achieve an even and balanced development of the international community under the existing international economic order. The gap between the developed and the developing countries continues to widen in a system which was established at a time when most of the developing countries did not even exist as independent States and which perpetuates inequality.

2. The present international economic order is in direct conflict with current developments in international political and economic relations. Since 1970, the world economy has experienced a series of grave crises which have had severe repercussions, especially on the developing countries because of their generally greater vulnerability to external economic impulses. The developing world has become a powerful factor that makes its influence felt in all fields of international activity. These irreversible changes in the relationship of forces in the world necessitate the active, full and equal participation of the developing countries in the formulation and application of all decisions that concern the international community.

3. All these changes have thrust into prominence the reality of interdependence of all the members of the world community. Current events have brought into sharp focus the realization that the interests of the developed countries and those of the developing countries can no longer be isolated from each other, that there is a close interrelationship between the prosperity of the developed countries and the growth and development of the developing countries, and that the prosperity of the international community as a whole depends upon the prosperity of its constituent parts. International co-operation for development is the shared goal and common duty of all countries. Thus the political, economic and social well-being of present and future generations depends more than ever on co-operation between all the

members of the international community on the basis of sovereign equality and the removal of the disequilibrium that exists between them.

4. The new international economic order should be founded on full respect for the following principles:

(*a*) Sovereign equality of States, self-determination of all peoples, inadmissibility of the acquisition of territories by force, territorial integrity and non-interference in the internal affairs of other States;

(*b*) The broadest co-operation of all the States members of the international community, based on equity, whereby the prevailing disparities in the world may be banished and prosperity secured for all;

(*c*) Full and effective participation on the basis of equality of all countries in the solving of world economic problems in the common interest of all countries, bearing in mind the necessity to ensure the accelerated development of all the developing countries, while devoting particular attention to the adoption of special measures in favour of the least developed, land-locked and island developing countries as well as those developing countries most seriously affected by economic crises and natural calamities, without losing sight of the interests of other developing countries;

(*d*) The right of every country to adopt the economic and social system that it deems the most appropriate for its own development and not to be subjected to discrimination of any kind as a result;

(*e*) Full permanent sovereignty of every State over its natural resources and all economic activities. In order to safeguard these resources, each State is entitled to exercise effective control over them and their exploitation with means suitable to its own situation, including the right to nationalization or transfer of ownership to its nationals, this right being an expression of the full permanent sovereignty of the State. No State may be subjected to economic, political or any other type of coercion to prevent the free and full exercise of this inalienable right;

(*f*) The right of all States, territories and peoples under foreign occupation, alien and colonial domination or *apartheid* to restitution and full compensation for the exploitation and depletion of, and damages to, the natural resources and all other resources of those States, territories and peoples;

(*g*) Regulation and supervision of the activities of transnational corporations by taking measures in the interest of the national economies of the countries where such transnational corporations operate on the basis of the full sovereignty of those countries;

(*h*) The right of the developing countries and the peoples of territories under colonial and racial domination and foreign occupation to achieve their liberation and to regain effective control over their natural resources and economic activities;

(*i*) The extending of assistance to developing countries, peoples and territories which are under colonial and alien domination, foreign occupation, racial discrimination or *apartheid* or are subjected to economic, political or any other type of coercive measures to obtain from them the subordination of the exercise of their sovereign rights and to secure from them advantages of any kind, and to neo-colonialism in all its forms, and which have established or are endeavouring to establish effective control over their natural resources and economic activities that have been or are still under foreign control;

(*j*) Just and equitable relationship between the prices of raw materials, primary commodities, manufactured and semi-manufactured goods exported by developing countries and the prices of raw materials, primary commodities, manufactures, capital goods and equipment imported by them with the aim of bringing about sustained improvement in their unsatisfactory terms of trade and the expansion of the world economy;

(*k*) Extension of active assistance to developing countries by the whole international community, free of any political or military conditions;

(*l*) Ensuring that one of the main aims of the reformed international monetary system shall be the promotion of the development of the developing countries and the adequate flow of real resources to them;

(*m*) Improving the competitiveness of natural materials facing competition from synthetic substitutes;

(*n*) Preferential and non-reciprocal treatment for developing countries, wherever feasible, in all fields of international economic co-operation whenever possible;

(*o*) Securing favourable conditions for the transfer of financial resources to developing countries;

(*p*) Giving to the developing countries access to the achievements of modern science and technology, and promoting the transfer of technology and the creation of indigenous technology for the benefit of the developing countries in forms and in accordance with procedures which are suited to their economies;

(*q*) The need for all States to put an end to the waste of natural resources, including food products;

(*r*) The need for developing countries to concentrate all their resources for the cause of development;

(*s*) The strengthening, through individual and collective actions, of mutual economic, trade, financial and technical co-operation among the developing countries, mainly on a preferential basis;

(*t*) Facilitating the role which producers' associations may play within the framework of international co-operation and, in pursuance of their aims, *inter alia* assisting in the promotion of sustained growth of the world economy and accelerating the development of developing countries.

5. The unanimous adoption of the International Development Strategy for the Second United Nations Development Decade[5] was an important step in the promotion of international economic co-operation on a just and equitable basis. The accelerated implementation of obligations and commitments assumed by the international community within the framework of the Strategy, particularly those concerning imperative development needs of developing countries, would contribute significantly to the fulfilment of the aims and objectives of the present Declaration.

6. The United Nations as a universal organization should be capable of dealing with problems of international economic co-operation in a compre-

---

[5] Resolution 2626 (XXV).

hensive manner and ensuring equally the interests of all countries. It must have an even greater role in the establishment of a new international economic order. The Charter of Economic Rights and Duties of States, for the preparation of which the present Declaration will provide an additional source of inspiration, will constitute a significant contribution in this respect. All the States Members of the United Nations are therefore called upon to exert maximum efforts with a view to securing the implementation of the present Declaration, which is one of the principal guarantees for the creation of better conditions for all peoples to reach a life worthy of human dignity.

7. The present Declaration on the Establishment of a New International Economic Order shall be one of the most important bases of economic relations between all peoples and all nations.

2229th plenary meeting
1 May 1974

3202 (S-VI). Programme of Action on the Establishment of a New International Economic Order

The General Assembly

Adopts the following Programme of Action:

PROGRAMME OF ACTION ON THE ESTABLISHMENT OF A NEW INTERNATIONAL ECONOMIC ORDER

CONTENTS

INTRODUCTION

1. In view of the continuing severe economic imbalance in the relations between developed and developing countries, and in the context of the constant and continuing aggravation of the imbalance of the economies of the developing countries and the consequent need for the mitigation of their current economic difficulties, urgent and effective measures need to be taken by the international community to assist the developing countries, while devoting particular attention to the least developed, land-locked and island developing countries and those developing countries most seriously affected by economic crises and natural calamities leading to serious retardation of development processes.

2. With a view to ensuring the application of the Declaration on the Establishment of a New International Economic Order,[6] it will be necessary to adopt and implement within a specified period a programme of action of unprecedented scope and to bring about maximum economic co-operation and understanding among all States, particularly between developed and developing countries, based on the principles of dignity and sovereign equality.

I. FUNDAMENTAL PROBLEMS OF RAW MATERIALS AND PRIMARY COMMODITIES AS RELATED TO TRADE AND DEVELOPMENT

1. *Raw materials*

All efforts should be made:

(a) To put an end to all forms of foreign occupation, racial discrimination, *apartheid*, colonial, neocolonial and alien domination and exploitation through the exercise of permanent sovereignty over natural resources;

(b) To take measures for the recovery, exploitation, development, marketing and distribution of natural resources, particularly of developing countries, to serve their national interests, to promote collective self-reliance among them and to strengthen mutually beneficial international economic co-operation with a view to bringing about the accelerated development of developing countries;

(c) To facilitate the functioning and to further the aims of producers' associations, including their joint marketing arrangements, orderly commodity trading, improvement in the export income of producing developing countries and in their terms of trade, and sustained growth of the world economy for the benefit of all;

(d) To evolve a just and equitable relationship between the prices of raw materials, primary commodities, manufactured and semi-manufactured goods exported by developing countries and the prices of raw materials, primary commodities, food, manufactured and semi-manufactured goods and capital equipment imported by them, and to work for a link between the prices of exports of developing countries and the prices of their imports from developed countries;

(e) To take measures to reverse the continued trend of stagnation or decline in the real price of several commodities exported by developing countries, despite a general rise in commodity prices, resulting in a decline in the export earnings of these developing countries;

(f) To take measures to expand the markets for natural products in relation to synthetics, taking into account the interests of the developing countries, and to utilize fully the ecological advantages of these products;

(g) To take measures to promote the processing of raw materials in the producer developing countries.

2. *Food*

All efforts should be made:

(a) To take full account of specific problems of developing countries, particularly in times of food

_____
[6] Resolution 3201 (S-VI).

shortages, in the international efforts connected with the food problem;

(*b*) To take into account that, owing to lack of means, some developing countries have vast potentialities of unexploited or underexploited land which, if reclaimed and put into practical use, would contribute considerably to the solution of the food crisis;

(*c*) By the international community to undertake concrete and speedy measures with a view to arresting desertification, salination and damage by locusts or any other similar phenomenon involving several developing countries, particularly in Africa, and gravely affecting the agricultural production capacity of these countries, and also to assist the developing countries affected by any such phenomenon to develop the affected zones with a view to contributing to the solution of their food problems;

(*d*) To refrain from damaging or deteriorating natural resources and food resources, especially those derived from the sea, by preventing pollution and taking appropriate steps to protect and reconstitute those resources;

(*e*) By developed countries, in evolving their policies relating to production, stocks, imports and exports of food, to take full account of the interests of:

(i) Developing importing countries which cannot afford high prices for their imports;

(ii) Developing exporting countries which need increased market opportunities for their exports;

(*f*) To ensure that developing countries can import the necessary quantity of food without undue strain on their foreign exchange resources and without unpredictable deterioration in their balance of payments, and, in this context, that special measures are taken in respect of the least developed, land-locked and island developing countries as well as those developing countries most seriously affected by economic crises and natural calamities;

(*g*) To ensure that concrete measures to increase food production and storage facilities in developing countries are introduced, *inter alia*, by ensuring an increase in all available essential inputs, including fertilizers, from developed countries on favourable terms;

(*h*) To promote exports of food products of developing countries through just and equitable arrangements, *inter alia*, by the progressive elimination of such protective and other measures as constitute unfair competition.

3. *General trade*

All efforts should be made:

(*a*) To take the following measures for the amelioration of terms of trade of developing countries and concrete steps to eliminate chronic trade deficits of developing countries:

(i) Fulfilment of relevant commitments already undertaken in the United Nations Conference on Trade and Development and in the International Development Strategy for the Second United Nations Development Decade;[7]

(ii) Improved access to markets in developed countries through the progressive removal of tariff and non-tariff barriers and of restrictive business practices;

---

[7] Resolution 2626 (XXV).

(iii) Expeditious formulation of commodity agreements where appropriate, in order to regulate as necessary and to stabilize the world markets for raw materials and primary commodities;

(iv) Preparation of an over-all integrated programme, setting out guidelines and taking into account the current work in this field, for a comprehensive range of commodities of export interest to developing countries;

(v) Where products of developing countries compete with the domestic production in developed countries, each developed country should facilitate the expansion of imports from developing countries and provide a fair and reasonable opportunity to the developing countries to share in the growth of the market;

(vi) When the importing developed countries derive receipts from customs duties, taxes and other protective measures applied to imports of these products, consideration should be given to the claim of the developing countries that these receipts should be reimbursed in full to the exporting developing countries or devoted to providing additional resources to meet their development needs;

(vii) Developed countries should make appropriate adjustments in their economies so as to facilitate the expansion and diversification of imports from developing countries and thereby permit a rational, just and equitable international division of labour;

(viii) Setting up general principles for pricing policy for exports of commodities of developing countries, with a view to rectifying and achieving satisfactory terms of trade for them;

(ix) Until satisfactory terms of trade are achieved for all developing countries, consideration should be given to alternative means, including improved compensatory financing schemes for meeting the development needs of the developing countries concerned;

(x) Implementation, improvement and enlargement of the generalized system of preferences for exports of agricultural primary commodities, manufactures and semi-manufactures from developing to developed countries and consideration of its extension to commodities, including those which are processed or semi-processed; developing countries which are or will be sharing their existing tariff advantages in some developed countries as the result of the introduction and eventual enlargement of the generalized system of preferences should, as a matter of urgency, be granted new openings in the markets of other developed countries which should offer them export opportunities that at least compensate for the sharing of those advantages;

(xi) The setting up of buffer stocks within the framework of commodity arrangements and their financing by international financial institutions, wherever necessary, by the developed countries and, when they are able to do so, by the developing countries, with the aim of favouring the producer developing and consumer developing countries and of contributing to the expansion of world trade as a whole;

(xii) In cases where natural materials can satisfy the requirements of the market, new investment for the expansion of the capacity to produce synthetic materials and substitutes should not be made;

(b) To be guided by the principles of non-reciprocity and preferential treatment of developing countries in multilateral trade negotiations between developed and developing countries, and to seek sustained and additional benefits for the international trade of developing countries, so as to achieve a substantial increase in their foreign exchange earnings, diversification of their exports and acceleration of the rate of their economic growth.

4. *Transportation and insurance*

All efforts should be made:

(a) To promote an increasing and equitable participation of developing countries in the world shipping tonnage;

(b) To arrest and reduce the ever-increasing freight rates in order to reduce the costs of imports to, and exports from, the developing countries;

(c) To minimize the cost of insurance and re-insurance for developing countries and to assist the growth of domestic insurance and reinsurance markets in developing countries and the establishment to this end, where appropriate, of institutions in these countries or at the regional level;

(d) To ensure the early implementation of the code of conduct for liner conferences;

(e) To take urgent measures to increase the import and export capability of the least developed countries and to offset the disadvantages of the adverse geographic situation of land-locked countries, particularly with regard to their transportation and transit costs, as well as developing island countries in order to increase their trading ability;

(f) By the developed countries to refrain from imposing measures or implementing policies designed to prevent the importation, at equitable prices, of commodities from the developing countries or from frustrating the implementation of legitimate measures and policies adopted by the developing countries in order to improve prices and encourage the export of such commodities.

II. INTERNATIONAL MONETARY SYSTEM AND FINANCING OF THE DEVELOPMENT OF DEVELOPING COUNTRIES

1. *Objectives*

All efforts should be made to reform the international monetary system with, *inter alia*, the following objectives:

(a) Measures to check the inflation already experienced by the developed countries, to prevent it from being transferred to developing countries and to study and devise possible arrangements within the International Monetary Fund to mitigate the effects of inflation in developed countries on the economies of developing countries;

(b) Measures to eliminate the instability of the international monetary system, in particular the uncertainty of the exchange rates, especially as it affects adversely the trade in commodities;

(c) Maintenance of the real value of the currency reserves of the developing countries by preventing their erosion from inflation and exchange rate depreciation of reserve currencies;

(d) Full and effective participation of developing countries in all phases of decision-making for the formulation of an equitable and durable monetary system and adequate participation of developing countries in all bodies entrusted with this reform and, particularly, in the proposed Council of Governors of the International Monetary Fund;

(e) Adequate and orderly creation of additional liquidity with particular regard to the needs of the developing countries through the additional allocation of special drawing rights based on the concept of world liquidity needs to be appropriately revised in the light of the new international environment; any creation of international liquidity should be made through international multilateral mechanisms;

(f) Early establishment of a link between special drawing rights and additional development financing in the interest of developing countries, consistent with the monetary characteristics of special drawing rights;

(g) Review by the International Monetary Fund of the relevant provisions in order to ensure effective participation by developing countries in the decision-making process;

(h) Arrangements to promote an increasing net transfer of real resources from the developed to the developing countries;

(i) Review of the methods of operation of the International Monetary Fund, in particular the terms for both credit repayments and "stand-by" arrangements, the system of compensatory financing, and the terms of the financing of commodity buffer stocks, so as to enable the developing countries to make more effective use of them.

2. *Measures*

All efforts should be made to take the following urgent measures to finance the development of developing countries and to meet the balance-of-payment crises in the developing world:

(a) Implementation at an accelerated pace by the developed countries of the time-bound programme, as already laid down in the International Development Strategy for the Second United Nations Development Decade, for the net amount of financial resource transfers to developing countries; increase in the official component of the net amount of financial resource transfers to developing countries so as to meet and even to exceed the target of the Strategy;

(b) International financing institutions should effectively play their role as development financing banks without discrimination on account of the political or economic system of any member country, assistance being untied;

(c) More effective participation by developing countries, whether recipients or contributors, in the decision-making process in the competent organs of the International Bank for Reconstruction and Development and the International Development Association, through the establishment of a more equitable pattern of voting rights;

(d) Exemption, wherever possible, of the developing countries from all import and capital outflow controls imposed by the developed countries;

(e) Promotion of foreign investment, both public and private, from developed to developing countries in accordance with the needs and requirements in sectors of their economies as determined by the recipient countries;

(f) Appropriate urgent measures, including international action, should be taken to mitigate adverse consequences for the current and future development of developing countries arising from the burden of external debt contracted on hard terms;

(g) Debt renegotiation on a case-by-case basis with a view to concluding agreements on debt cancellation, moratorium, rescheduling or interest subsidization;

(h) International financial institutions should take into account the special situation of each developing country in reorienting their lending policies to suit these urgent needs; there is also need for improvement in practices of international financial institutions in regard to, *inter alia*, development financing and international monetary problems;

(i) Appropriate steps should be taken to give priority to the least developed, land-locked and island developing countries and to the countries most seriously affected by economic crises and natural calamities, in the availability of loans for development purposes which should include more favourable terms and conditions.

III. INDUSTRIALIZATION

All efforts should be made by the international community to take measures to encourage the industrialization of the developing countries, and to this end:

(a) The developed countries should respond favourably, within the framework of their official aid as well as international financial institutions, to the requests of developing countries for the financing of industrial projects;

(b) The developed countries should encourage investors to finance industrial production projects, particularly export-oriented production, in developing countries, in agreement with the latter and within the context of their laws and regulations;

(c) With a view to bringing about a new international economic structure which should increase the share of the developing countries in world industrial production, the developed countries and the agencies of the United Nations system, in co-operation with the developing countries, should contribute to setting up new industrial capacities including raw materials and commodity-transforming facilities as a matter of priority in the developing countries that produce those raw materials and commodities;

(d) The international community should continue and expand, with the aid of the developed countries and the international institutions, the operational and instruction-oriented technical assistance programmes, including vocational training and management development of national personnel of the developing countries, in the light of their special development requirements.

IV. TRANSFER OF TECHNOLOGY

All efforts should be made:

(a) To formulate an international code of conduct for the transfer of technology corresponding to needs and conditions prevalent in developing countries;

(b) To give access on improved terms to modern technology and to adapt that technology, as appropriate, to specific economic, social and ecological conditions and varying stages of development in developing countries;

(c) To expand significantly the assistance from developed to developing countries in research and development programmes and in the creation of suitable indigenous technology;

(d) To adapt commercial practices governing transfer of technology to the requirements of the developing countries and to prevent abuse of the rights of sellers;

(e) To promote international co-operation in research and development in exploration and exploitation, conservation and the legitimate utilization of natural resources and all sources of energy.

In taking the above measures, the special needs of the least developed and land-locked countries should be borne in mind.

V. REGULATION AND CONTROL OVER THE ACTIVITIES OF TRANSNATIONAL CORPORATIONS

All efforts should be made to formulate, adopt and implement an international code of conduct for transnational corporations:

(a) To prevent interference in the internal affairs of the countries where they operate and their collaboration with racist régimes and colonial administrations;

(b) To regulate their activities in host countries, to eliminate restrictive business practices and to conform to the national development plans and objectives of developing countries, and in this context facilitate, as necessary, the review and revision of previously concluded arrangements;

(c) To bring about assistance, transfer of technology and management skills to developing countries on equitable and favourable terms;

(d) To regulate the repatriation of the profits accruing from their operations, taking into account the legitimate interests of all parties concerned;

(e) To promote reinvestment of their profits in developing countries.

VI. CHARTER OF ECONOMIC RIGHTS AND DUTIES OF STATES

The Charter of Economic Rights and Duties of States, the draft of which is being prepared by a working group of the United Nations and which the General Assembly has already expressed the intention of adopting at its twenty-ninth regular session, shall constitute an effective instrument towards the establishment of a new system of international economic relations based on equity, sovereign equality, and interdependence of the interests of developed and developing countries. It is therefore of vital importance that the aforementioned Charter be adopted by the General Assembly at its twenty-ninth session.

VII. PROMOTION OF CO-OPERATION AMONG DEVELOPING COUNTRIES

1. Collective self-reliance and growing co-operation among developing countries will further strengthen their role in the new international economic order. Developing countries, with a view to expanding co-operation at the regional, subregional and interregional levels, should take further steps, *inter alia*:

(a) To support the establishment and/or improvement of an appropriate mechanism to defend the prices of their exportable commodities and to improve access to and stabilize markets for them. In this context the increasingly effective mobilization by the whole group of oil-exporting countries of their natural resources for the benefit of their economic development is to be welcomed. At the same time there is the paramount need for co-operation among the developing countries in evolving urgently and in a spirit of solidarity all possible means to assist developing countries to cope with the immediate problems resulting from this legitimate and perfectly justified action. The measures already taken in this regard are a positive indication of the evolving co-operation between developing countries;

(b) To protect their inalienable right to permanent sovereignty over their natural resources;

(c) To promote, establish or strengthen economic integration at the regional and subregional levels;

(d) To increase considerably their imports from other developing countries;

(e) To ensure that no developing country accords to imports from developed countries more favourable treatment than that accorded to imports from developing countries. Taking into account the existing international agreements, current limitations and possibilities and also their future evolution, preferential treatment should be given to the procurement of import requirements from other developing countries. Wherever possible, preferential treatment should be given to imports from developing countries and the exports of those countries;

(f) To promote close co-operation in the fields of finance, credit relations and monetary issues, including the development of credit relations on a preferential basis and on favourable terms;

(g) To strengthen efforts which are already being made by developing countries to utilize available financial resources for financing development in the developing countries through investment, financing of export-oriented and emergency projects and other long-term assistance;

(h) To promote and establish effective instruments of co-operation in the fields of industry, science and technology, transport, shipping and mass communication media.

2. Developed countries should support initiatives in the regional, subregional and interregional co-operation of developing countries through the extension of financial and technical assistance by more effective and concrete actions, particularly in the field of commercial policy.

VIII. ASSISTANCE IN THE EXERCISE OF PERMANENT SOVEREIGNTY OF STATES OVER NATURAL RESOURCES

All efforts should be made:

(a) To defeat attempts to prevent the free and effective exercise of the rights of every State to full and permanent sovereignty over its natural resources;

(b) To ensure that competent agencies of the United Nations system meet requests for assistance from developing countries in connexion with the operation of nationalized means of production.

IX. STRENGTHENING THE ROLE OF THE UNITED NATIONS SYSTEM IN THE FIELD OF INTERNATIONAL ECONOMIC CO-OPERATION

1. In furtherance of the objectives of the International Development Strategy for the Second United Nations Development Decade and in accordance with the aims and objectives of the Declaration on the Establishment of a New International Economic Order, all Member States pledge to make full use of the United Nations system in the implementation of the present Programme of Action, jointly adopted by them, in working for the establishment of a new international economic order and thereby strengthening the role of the United Nations in the field of world-wide co-operation for economic and social development.

2. The General Assembly of the United Nations shall conduct an over-all review of the implementation of the Programme of Action as a priority item. All the activities of the United Nations system to be undertaken under the Programme of Action as well as those already planned, such as the World Population Conference, 1974, the World Food Conference, the Second General Conference of the United Nations Industrial Development Organization and the mid-term. review and appraisal of the International Development Strategy for the Second United Nations Development Decade should be so directed as to enable the special session of the General Assembly on development, called for under Assembly resolution 3172 (XXVIII) of 17 December 1973, to make its full contribution to the establishment of the new international economic order. All Member States are urged, jointly and individually, to direct their efforts and policies towards the success of that special session.

3. The Economic and Social Council shall define the policy framework and co-ordinate the activities of all organizations, institutions and subsidiary bodies within the United Nations system which shall be entrusted with the task of implementing the present Programme of Action. In order to enable the Economic and Social Council to carry out its tasks effectively:

(a) All organizations, institutions and subsidiary bodies concerned within the United Nations system shall submit to the Economic and Social Council progress reports on the implementation of the Programme of Action within their respective fields of competence as often as necessary, but not less than once a year;

(b) The Economic and Social Council shall examine the progress reports as a matter of urgency, to which end it may be convened, as necessary, in special session or, if need be, may function continuously. It shall draw the attention of the General Assembly to the problems and difficulties arising in connexion with the implementation of the Programme of Action.

4. All organizations, institutions, subsidiary bodies and conferences of the United Nations system are entrusted with the implementation of the Programme of Action. The activities of the United Nations Conference on Trade and Development, as set forth in General Assembly resolution 1995 (XIX) of 30 December 1964, should be strengthened for the purpose of following in collaboration with other competent organizations the development of international trade in raw materials throughout the world.

5. Urgent and effective measures should be taken to review the lending policies of international financial institutions, taking into account the special situation of each developing country, to suit urgent needs, to improve the practices of these institutions in regard to, *inter alia*, development financing and international monetary problems, and to ensure more effective participation by developing countries—whether recipients or contributors—in the decision-making process through appropriate revision of the pattern of voting rights.

6. The developed countries and others in a position to do so should contribute substantially to the various organizations, programmes and funds established within the United Nations system for the purpose of accelerating economic and social development in developing countries.

7. The present Programme of Action complements and strengthens the goals and objectives embodied in the International Development Strategy for the Second United Nations Development Decade as well as the new measures formulated by the General Assembly at its twenty-eighth session to offset the shortfalls in achieving those goals and objectives.

8. The implementation of the Programme of Action should be taken into account at the time of the mid-term review and appraisal of the International Development Strategy for the Second United Nations Development Decade. New commitments, changes, additions and adaptations in the Strategy should be made, as appropriate, taking into account the Declaration on the Establishment of a New International Economic Order and the present Programme of Action.

X. SPECIAL PROGRAMME

The General Assembly adopts the following Special Programme, including particularly emergency measures to mitigate the difficulties of the developing countries most seriously affected by economic crisis, bearing in mind the particular problem of the least developed and land-locked countries:

The General Assembly,

Taking into account the following considerations:

(*a*) The sharp increase in the prices of their essential imports such as food, fertilizers, energy products, capital goods, equipment and services, including transportation and transit costs, has gravely exacerbated the increasingly adverse terms of trade of a number of developing countries, added to the burden of their foreign debt and, cumulatively, created a situation which, if left untended, will make it impossible for them to finance their essential imports and development and result in a further deterioration in the levels and conditions of life in these countries. The present crisis is the outcome of all the problems that

have accumulated over the years: in the field of trade, in monetary reform, the world-wide inflationary situation, inadequacy and delay in provision of financial assistance and many other similar problems in the economic and developmental fields. In facing the crisis, this complex situation must be borne in mind so as to ensure that the Special Programme adopted by the international community provides emergency relief and timely assistance to the most seriously affected countries. Simultaneously, steps are being taken to resolve these outstanding problems through a fundamental restructuring of the world economic system, in order to allow these countries while solving the present difficulties to reach an acceptable level of development.

(*b*) The special measures adopted to assist the most seriously affected countries must encompass not only the relief which they require on an emergency basis to maintain their import requirements, but also, beyond that, steps to consciously promote the capacity of these countries to produce and earn more. Unless such a comprehensive approach is adopted, there is every likelihood that the difficulties of the most seriously affected countries may be perpetuated. Nevertheless, the first and most pressing task of the international community is to enable these countries to meet the shortfall in their balance-of-payments positions. But this must be simultaneously supplemented by additional development assistance to maintain and thereafter accelerate their rate of economic development.

(*c*) The countries which have been most seriously affected are precisely those which are at the greatest disadvantage in the world economy: the least developed, the land-locked and other low-income developing countries as well as other developing countries whose economies have been seriously dislocated as a result of the present economic crisis, natural calamities, and foreign aggression and occupation. An indication of the countries thus affected, the level of the impact on their economies and the kind of relief and assistance they require can be assessed on the basis, *inter alia*, of the following criteria:

 (i) Low *per capita* income as a reflection of relative poverty, low productivity, low level of technology and development;

 (ii) Sharp increase in their import cost of essentials relative to export earnings;

 (iii) High ratio of debt servicing to export earnings;

 (iv) Insufficiency in export earnings, comparative inelasticity of export incomes and unavailability of exportable surplus;

 (v) Low level of foreign exchange reserves or their inadequacy for requirements;

 (vi) Adverse impact of higher transportation and transit costs;

 (vii) Relative importance of foreign trade in the development process.

(*d*) The assessment of the extent and nature of the impact on the economies of the most seriously affected countries must be made flexible, keeping in mind the present uncertainty in the world economy, the adjustment policies that may be adopted by the developed countries and the flow of capital and investment. Estimates of the payments situation and needs of these countries can be assessed and projected reliably only on the basis of their average performance over a number of years. Long-term projections, at this time, cannot but be uncertain.

(*e*) It is important that, in the special measures to mitigate the difficulties of the most seriously affected countries, all the developed countries as well as the developing countries should contribute according to their level of development and the capacity and strength of their economies. It is notable that some developing countries, despite their own difficulties and development needs, have shown a willingness to play a concrete and helpful role in ameliorating the difficulties faced by the poorer developing countries. The various initiatives and measures taken recently by certain developing countries with adequate resources on a bilateral and multilateral basis to contribute to alleviating the difficulties of other developing countries are a reflection of their commitment to the principle of effective economic co-operation among developing countries.

(*f*) The response of the developed countries which have by far the greater capacity to assist the affected countries in overcoming their present difficulties must be commensurate with their responsibilities. Their assistance should be in addition to the presently available levels of aid. They should fulfil and if possible exceed the targets of the International Development Strategy for the Second United Nations Development Decade on financial assistance to the developing countries, especially that relating to official development assistance. They should also give serious consideration to the cancellation of the external debts of the most seriously affected countries. This would provide the simplest and quickest relief to the affected countries. Favourable consideration should also be given to debt moratorium and rescheduling. The current situation should not lead the industrialized countries to adopt what will ultimately prove to be a self-defeating policy aggravating the present crisis.

Recalling the constructive proposals made by His Imperial Majesty the Shahanshah of Iran[8] and His Excellency Mr. Houari Boumediène, President of the People's Democratic Republic of Algeria,[9]

1. *Decides* to launch a Special Programme to provide emergency relief and development assistance to the developing countries most seriously affected, as a matter of urgency, and for the period of time necessary, at least until the end of the Second United Nations Development Decade, to help them overcome their present difficulties and to achieve self-sustaining economic development;

2. *Decides* as a first step in the Special Programme to request the Secretary-General to launch an emergency operation to provide timely relief to the most seriously affected developing countries, as defined in subparagraph (*c*) above, with the aim of maintaining unimpaired essential imports for the duration of the coming twelve months and to invite the indus-

[8] A/9548, annex.
[9] *Official Records of the General Assembly, Sixth Special Session, Plenary Meetings,* 2208th meeting, paras. 3-152.

trialized countries and other potential contributors to announce their contributions for emergency assistance, or intimate their intention to do so, by 15 June 1974 to be provided through bilateral or multilateral channels, taking into account the commitments and measures of assistance announced or already taken by some countries, and further requests the Secretary-General to report the progress of the emergency operation to the General Assembly at its twenty-ninth session, through the Economic and Social Council at its fifty-seventh session;

3. *Calls upon* the industrialized countries and other potential contributors to extend to the most seriously affected countries immediate relief and assistance which must be of an order of magnitude that is commensurate with the needs of these countries. Such assistance should be in addition to the existing level of aid and provided at a very early date to the maximum possible extent on a grant basis and, where not possible, on soft terms. The disbursement and relevant operational procedures and terms must reflect this exceptional situation. The assistance could be provided either through bilateral or multilateral channels, including such new institutions and facilities that have been or are to be set up. The special measures may include the following:

(*a*) Special arrangements on particularly favourable terms and conditions including possible subsidies for and assured supplies of essential commodities and goods;

(*b*) Deferred payments for all or part of imports of essential commodities and goods;

(*c*) Commodity assistance, including food aid, on a grant basis or deferred payments in local currencies, bearing in mind that this should not adversely affect the exports of developing countries;

(*d*) Long-term suppliers' credits on easy terms;

(*e*) Long-term financial assistance on concessionary terms;

(*f*) Drawings from special International Monetary Fund facilities on concessional terms;

(*g*) Establishment of a link between the creation of special drawing rights and development assistance, taking into account the additional financial requirements of the most seriously affected countries;

(*h*) Subsidies, provided bilaterally or multilaterally, for interest on funds available on commercial terms borrowed by the most seriously affected countries;

(*i*) Debt renegotiation on a case-by-case basis with a view to concluding agreements on debt cancellation, moratorium or rescheduling;

(*j*) Provision on more favourable terms of capital goods and technical assistance to accelerate the industrialization of the affected countries;

(*k*) Investment in industrial and development projects on favourable terms;

(*l*) Subsidizing the additional transit and transport costs, especially of the land-locked countries;

4. *Appeals* to the developed countries to consider favourably the cancellation, moratorium or rescheduling of the debts of the most seriously affected developing countries, on their request, as an important contribution to mitigating the grave and urgent difficulties of these countries;

5. *Decides* to establish a Special Fund under the auspices of the United Nations, through voluntary contributions from industrialized countries and other potential contributors, as a part of the Special Programme, to provide emergency relief and development assistance, which will commence its operations at the latest by 1 January 1975;

6. *Establishes* an *Ad Hoc* Committee on the Special Programme, composed of thirty-six Member States appointed by the President of the General Assembly, after appropriate consultations, bearing in mind the purposes of the Special Fund and its terms of reference:

(*a*) To make recommendations, *inter alia*, on the scope, machinery and modes of operation of the Special Fund, taking into account the need for:

(i) Equitable representation on its governing body;

(ii) Equitable distribution of its resources;

(iii) Full utilization of the services and facilities of existing international organizations;

(iv) The possibility of merging the United Nations Capital Development Fund with the operations of the Special Fund;

(v) A central monitoring body to oversee the various measures being taken both bilaterally and multilaterally;

and, to this end, bearing in mind the different ideas and proposals submitted at the sixth special session, including those put forward by Iran[10] and those made at the 2208th plenary meeting, and the comments thereon, and the possibility of utilizing the Special Fund to provide an alternative channel for normal development assistance after the emergency period;

(*b*) To monitor, pending commencement of the operations of the Special Fund, the various measures being taken both bilaterally and multilaterally to assist the most seriously affected countries;

(*c*) To prepare, on the basis of information provided by the countries concerned and by appropriate agencies of the United Nations system, a broad assessment of:

(i) The magnitude of the difficulties facing the most seriously affected countries;

(ii) The kind and quantities of the commodities and goods essentially required by them;

(iii) Their need for financial assistance;

(iv) Their technical assistance requirements, including especially access to technology;

7. *Requests* the Secretary-General of the United Nations, the Secretary-General of the United Nations Conference on Trade and Development, the President of the International Bank for Reconstruction and Development, the Managing Director of the International Monetary Fund, the Administrator of the United Nations Development Programme and the heads of the other competent international organizations to assist the *Ad Hoc* Committee on the Special Programme in performing the functions assigned to it under paragraph 6 above, and to help, as appropriate, in the operations of the Special Fund;

8. *Requests* the International Monetary Fund to expedite decisions on:

(*a*) The establishment of an extended special facility with a view to enabling the most seriously affected developing countries to participate in it on favourable terms;

(*b*) The creation of special drawing rights and the early establishment of the link between their allocation and development financing;

(*c*) The establishment and operation of the proposed new special facility to extend credits and subsidize interest charges on commercial funds borrowed by Member States, bearing in mind the interests of the developing countries and especially the additional financial requirements of the most seriously affected countries;

9. *Requests* the World Bank Group and the International Monetary Fund to place their managerial, financial and technical services at the disposal of Governments contributing to emergency financial relief so as to enable them to assist without delay in channelling funds to the recipients, making such institutional and procedural changes as may be required;

10. *Invites* the United Nations Development Programme to take the necessary steps, particularly at the country level, to respond on an emergency basis to requests for additional assistance which it may be called upon to render within the framework of the Special Programme;

11. *Requests* the *Ad Hoc* Committee on the Special Programme to submit its report and recommendations to the Economic and Social Council at its fifty-seventh session and invites the Council, on the basis of its consideration of that report, to submit suitable recommendations to the General Assembly at its twenty-ninth session;

12. *Decides* to consider as a matter of high priority at its twenty-ninth session, within the framework of a new international economic order, the question of special measures for the most seriously affected countries.

2229th plenary meeting
1 May 1974

* *

The President of the General Assembly subsequently informed the Secretary-General[11] that, in pursuance of section X, paragraph 6, of the above resolution, he had appointed the members of the *Ad Hoc* Committee on the Special Programme.

As a result, the *Ad Hoc* Committee will be composed of the following Member States: ALGERIA, ARGENTINA, AUSTRALIA, BRAZIL, CHAD, COSTA RICA, CZECHOSLOVAKIA, FRANCE, GERMANY (FEDERAL REPUBLIC OF), GUYANA, INDIA, IRAN, JAPAN, KUWAIT, MADAGASCAR, NEPAL, NETHERLANDS, NIGERIA, NORWAY, PAKISTAN, PARAGUAY, PHILIPPINES, SOMALIA, SRI LANKA, SUDAN, SWAZILAND, SYRIAN ARAB REPUBLIC, TURKEY, UNION OF SOVIET SOCIALIST REPUBLICS, UNITED KINGDOM OF GREAT BRITAIN AND NORTHERN IRELAND, UNITED STATES OF AMERICA, UPPER VOLTA, URUGUAY, VENEZUELA, YUGOSLAVIA and ZAIRE.

---

[10] A/AC.166/L.15; see also A/9548, annex.

[11] A/9558 and Add.1.

119

RESOLUTION ON DEVELOPMENT
AND INTERNATIONAL COOPERATION

3362 (S-VII). Development and international economic co-operation

The General Assembly,

Determined to eliminate injustice and inequality which afflict vast sections of humanity and to accelerate the development of developing countries,

Recalling the Declaration and the Programme of Action on the Establishment of a New International Economic Order,[10] as well as the Charter of Economic Rights and Duties of States,[11] which lay down the foundations of the new international economic order.

Reaffirming the fundamental purposes of the abovementioned documents and the rights and duties of all States to seek and participate in the solutions of the problems afflicting the world, in particular the imperative need of redressing the economic imbalance between developed and developing countries,

Recalling further the International Development Strategy for the Second United Nations Development Decade,[12] which should be reviewed in the light of the Programme of Action on the Establishment of a New International Economic Order, and determined to implement the targets and policy measures contained in the International Development Strategy,

Conscious that the accelerated development of developing countries would be a decisive element for the promotion of world peace and security,

Recognizing that greater co-operation among States in the fields of trade, industry, science and technology as well as in other fields of economic activities, based on the principles of the Declaration and the Programme of Action on the Establishment of a New International Economic Order and of the Charter of Economic Rights and Duties of States, would also contribute to strengthening peace and security in the world,

Believing that the over-all objective of the new international economic order is to increase the capacity of developing countries, individually and collectively, to pursue their development,

Decides, to this end and in the context of the foregoing, to set in motion the following measures as the basis and framework for the work of the competent bodies and organizations of the United Nations system:

I. INTERNATIONAL TRADE

1. Concerted efforts should be made in favour of the developing countries towards expanding and diversifying their trade, improving and diversifying their productive capacity, improving their productivity and increasing their export earnings, with a view

to counteracting the adverse effects of inflation—thereby sustaining real incomes—and with a view to improving the terms of trade of the developing countries and in order to eliminate the economic imbalance between developed and developing countries.

2. Concerted action should be taken to accelerate the growth and diversification of the export trade of developing countries in manufactures and semi-manufactures and in processed and semi-processed products in order to increase their share in world industrial output and world trade within the framework of an expanding world economy.

3. An important aim of the fourth session of the United Nations Conference on Trade and Development, in addition to work in progress elsewhere, should be to reach decisions on the improvement of market structures in the field of raw materials and commodities of export interest to the developing countries, including decisions with respect to an integrated programme and the applicability of elements thereof. In this connexion, taking into account the distinctive features of individual raw materials and commodities, the decisions should bear on the following:

(*a*) Appropriate international stocking and other forms of market arrangements for securing stable, remunerative and equitable prices for commodities of export interest to developing countries and promoting equilibrium between supply and demand, including, where possible, long-term multilateral commitments;

(*b*) Adequate international financing facilities for such stocking and market arrangements;

(*c*) Where possible, promotion of long-term and medium-term contracts;

(*d*) Substantial improvement of facilities for compensatory financing of export revenue fluctuations through the widening and enlarging of the existing facilities. Note has been taken of the various proposals regarding a comprehensive scheme for the stabilization of export earnings of developing countries and for a development security facility as well as specific measures for the benefit of the developing countries most in need;

(*e*) Promotion of processing of raw materials in producing developing countries and expansion and diversification of their exports, particularly to developed countries;

(*f*) Effective opportunities to improve the share of developing countries in transport, marketing and distribution of their primary commodities and to encourage measures of world significance for the evolution of the infrastructure and secondary capacity of developing countries from the production of

[10] Resolutions 3201 (S-VI) and 3202 (S-VI).
[11] Resolution 3281 (XXIX).
[12] Resolution 2626 (XXV).

primary commodities to processing, transport and marketing, and to the production of finished manufactured goods, their transport, distribution and exchange, including advanced financial and exchange institutions for the remunerative management of trade transactions.

4. The Secretary-General of the United Nations Conference on Trade and Development should present a report to the Conference at its fourth session on the impact of an integrated programme on the imports of developing countries which are net importers of raw materials and commodities, including those lacking in natural resources, and recommend any remedial measures that may be necessary.

5. A number of options are open to the international community to preserve the purchasing power of developing countries. These need to be further studied on a priority basis. The Secretary-General of the United Nations Conference on Trade and Development should continue to study direct and indirect indexation schemes and other options with a view to making concrete proposals before the Conference at its fourth session.

6. The Secretary-General of the United Nations Conference on Trade and Development should prepare a preliminary study on the proportion between prices of raw materials and commodities exported by developing countries and the final consumer price, particularly in developed countries, and submit it, if possible, to the Conference at its fourth session.

7. Developed countries should fully implement agreed provisions on the principle of standstill as regards imports from developing countries, and any departure should be subjected to such measures as consultations and multilateral surveillance and compensation, in accordance with internationally agreed criteria and procedures.

8. Developed countries should take effective steps within the framework of multilateral trade negotiations for the reduction or removal, where feasible and appropriate, of non-tariff barriers affecting the products of export interest to developing countries on a differential and more favourable basis for developing countries. The generalized scheme of preferences should not terminate at the end of the period of ten years originally envisaged and should be continuously improved through wider coverage, deeper cuts and other measures, bearing in mind the interests of those developing countries which enjoy special advantages and the need for finding ways and means for protecting their interests.

9. Countervailing duties should be applied only in conformity with internationally agreed obligations. Developed countries should exercise maximum restraint within the framework of international obligations in the imposition of countervailing duties on the imports of products from developing countries. The multilateral trade negotiations under way should take fully into account the particular interests of developing countries with a view to providing them differential and more favourable treatment in appropriate cases.

10. Restrictive business practices adversely affecting international trade, particularly that of developing countries, should be eliminated and efforts should be made at the national and international levels with the objective of negotiating a set of equitable principles and rules.

11. Special measures should be undertaken by developed countries and by developing countries in a position to do so to assist in the structural transformation of the economy of the least developed, land-locked and island developing countries.

12. Emergency measures as spelled out in section X of General Assembly resolution 3202 (S-VI) should be undertaken on a temporary basis to meet the specific problems of the most seriously affected countries as defined in Assembly resolutions 3201 (S-VI) and 3202 (S-VI) of 1 May 1974, without any detriment to the interests of the developing countries as a whole.

13. Further expansion of trade between the socialist countries of Eastern Europe and the developing countries should be intensified as is provided for in resolutions 15 (II) of 25 March 1968[13] and 53 (III) of 19 May 1972[14] of the United Nations Conference on Trade and Development. Additional measures and appropriate orientation to achieve this end are necessary.

II. TRANSFER OF REAL RESOURCES FOR FINANCING THE DEVELOPMENT OF DEVELOPING COUNTRIES AND INTERNATIONAL MONETARY REFORMS

1. Concessional financial resources to developing countries need to be increased substantially, their terms and conditions ameliorated and their flow made predictable, continuous and increasingly assured so as to facilitate the implementation by developing countries of long-term programmes for economic and social development. Financial assistance should, as a general rule, be untied.

2. Developed countries confirm their continued commitment in respect of the targets relating to the transfer of resources, in particular the official development assistance target of 0.7 per cent of gross national product, as agreed in the International Development Strategy for the Second United Nations Development Decade, and adopt as their common aim an effective increase in official development assistance with a view to achieving these targets by the end of the decade. Developed countries which have not yet made a commitment in respect of these targets undertake to make their best efforts to reach these targets in the remaining part of this decade.

3. The establishment of a link between the special drawing rights and development assistance should form part of the consideration by the International Monetary Fund of the creation of new special drawing rights as and when they are created according to the needs of international liquidity. Agreement should be reached at an early date on the establishment of a trust fund, to be financed partly through the International Monetary Fund gold sales and partly through voluntary contributions and to be governed by an appropriate body, for the benefit of developing countries. Consideration of other means of transfer of real resources which are predictable, assured and continuous should be expedited in appropriate bodies.

---

[13] *Proceedings of the United Nations Conference on Trade and Development, Second Session,* vol. I and Corr.1 and 3 and Add.1 and 2, *Report and Annexes* (United Nations publication, Sales No. E.68.II.D.14), p. 32.

[14] See *Proceedings of the United Nations Conference on Trade and Development, Third Session,* vol. I, *Report and Annexes* (United Nations publication, Sales No. E.73.II.D.4), annex I.A.

4. Developed countries and international organizations should enhance the real value and volume of assistance to developing countries and ensure that the developing countries obtain the largest possible share in the procurement of equipment, consultants and consultancy services. Such assistance should be on softer terms and, as a general rule, untied.

5. In order to enlarge the pool of resources available for financing development, there is an urgent need to increase substantially the capital of the World Bank Group, in particular the resources of the International Development Association, to enable it to make additional capital available to the poorest countries on highly concessional terms.

6. The resources of the development institutions of the United Nations system, in particular the United Nations Development Programme, should also be increased. The funds at the disposal of the regional development banks should be augmented. These increases should be without prejudice to bilateral development assistance flows.

7. To the extent desirable, the World Bank Group is invited to consider new ways of supplementing its financing with private management, skills, technology and capital and also new approaches to increase financing of development in developing countries, in accordance with their national plans and priorities.

8. The burden of debt on developing countries is increasing to a point where the import capacity as well as reserves have come under serious strain. At its fourth session the United Nations Conference on Trade and Development shall consider the need for, and the possibility of, convening as soon as possible a conference of major donor, creditor and debtor countries to devise ways and means to mitigate this burden, taking into account the development needs of developing countries, with special attention to the plight of the most seriously affected countries as defined in General Assembly resolutions 3201 (S-VI) and 3202 (S-VI).

9. Developing countries should be granted increased access on favourable terms to the capital markets of developed countries. To this end, the joint Development Committee of the International Monetary Fund and the International Bank for Reconstruction and Development should progress as rapidly as possible in its work. Appropriate United Nations bodies and other related intergovernmental agencies should be invited to examine ways and means of increasing the flow of public and private resources to developing countries, including proposals made at the current session to provide investment in private and public enterprises in the developing countries. Consideration should be given to the examination of an international investment trust and to the expansion of the International Finance Corporation capital without prejudice to the increase in resources of other intergovernmental financial and development institutions and bilateral assistance flows.

10. Developed and developing countries should further co-operate through investment of financial resources and supply of technology and equipment to developing countries by developed countries and by developing countries in a position to do so.

11. Developed countries, and developing countries in a position to do so, are urged to make adequate contributions to the United Nations Special Fund with a view to an early implementation of a programme of lending, preferably in 1976.

12. Developed countries should improve terms and conditions of their assistance so as to include a preponderant grant element for the least developed, land-locked and island developing countries.

13. In providing additional resources for assisting the most seriously affected countries in helping them to meet their serious balance-of-payments deficits, all developed countries, and developing countries in a position to do so, and international organizations such as the International Bank for Reconstruction and Development and the International Monetary Fund, should undertake specific measures in their favour, including those provided in General Assembly resolutions 3201 (S-VI) and 3202 (S-VI).

14. Special attention should be given by the international community to the phenomena of natural disasters which frequently afflict many parts of the world, with far-reaching devastating economic, social and structural consequences, particularly in the least developed countries. To this end, the General Assembly at its thirtieth session, in considering this problem, should examine and adopt appropriate measures.

15. The role of national reserve currencies should be reduced and the special drawing rights should become the central reserve asset of the international monetary system in order to provide for greater international control over the creation and equitable distribution of liquidity and in order to limit potential losses as a consequence of exchange rate fluctuations. Arrangements for gold should be consistent with the agreed objective of reducing the role of gold in the system and with equitable distribution of new international liquidity and should in particular take into consideration the needs of developing countries for increased liquidity.

16. The process of decision-making should be fair and responsive to change and should be most specially responsive to the emergence of a new economic influence on the part of developing countries. The participation of developing countries in the decision-making process in the competent organs of international finance and development institutions should be adequately increased and made more effective without adversely affecting the broad geographic representation of developing countries and in accordance with the existing and evolving rules.

17. The compensatory financing facility now available through the International Monetary Fund should be expanded and liberalized. In this connexion, early consideration should be given by the Fund and other appropriate United Nations bodies to various proposals made at the current session—including the examination of a new development security facility—which would mitigate export earnings shortfalls of developing countries, with special regard to the poorest countries, and thus provide greater assistance to their continued economic development. Early consideration should also be given by the International Monetary Fund to proposals to expand and liberalize its coverage of current transactions to include manufactures and services, to ensure that, whenever possible, compensation for export shortfalls takes place at the same time they

occur, to take into account, in determining the quantum of compensation, movements in import prices and to lengthen the repayment period.

18. Drawing under the buffer stock financing facility of the International Monetary Fund should be accorded treatment with respect to floating alongside the gold tranche, similar to that under the compensatory financing facility, and the Fund should expedite its study of the possibility of an amendment of the Articles of Agreement, to be presented to the Interim Committee, if possible at its next meeting, that would permit the Fund to provide assistance directly to international buffer stocks of primary products.

III. SCIENCE AND TECHNOLOGY

1. Developed and developing countries should co-operate in the establishment, strengthening and development of the scientific and technological infrastructure of developing countries. Developed countries should also take appropriate measures, such as contribution to the establishment of an industrial technological information bank and consideration of the possibility of regional and sectoral banks, in order to make available a greater flow to developing countries of information permitting the selection of technologies, in particular advanced technologies. Consideration should also be given to the establishment of an international centre for the exchange of technological information for the sharing of research findings relevant to developing countries. For the above purposes institutional arrangements within the United Nations system should be examined by the General Assembly at its thirtieth session.

2. Developed countries should significantly expand their assistance to developing countries for direct support to their science and technology programmes, as well as increase substantially the proportion of their research and development devoted to specific problems of primary interest to developing countries, and in the creation of suitable indigenous technology, in accordance with feasible targets to be agreed upon. The General Assembly invites the Secretary-General to carry out a preliminary study and to report to the Assembly at its thirty-first session on the possibility of establishing, within the framework of the United Nations system, an international energy institute to assist all developing countries in energy resources research and development.

3. All States should co-operate in evolving an international code of conduct for the transfer of technology, corresponding, in particular, to the special needs of the developing countries. Work on such a code should therefore be continued within the United Nations Conference on Trade and Development and concluded in time for decisions to be reached at the fourth session of the Conference, including a decision on the legal character of such a code with the objective of the adoption of a code of conduct prior to the end of 1977. International conventions on patents and trade marks should be reviewed and revised to meet, in particular, the special needs of the developing countries, in order that these conventions may become more satisfactory instruments for aiding developing countries in the transfer and development of technology. National patents systems should, without delay, be brought into line with the international patent system in its revised form.

4. Developed countries should facilitate the access of developing countries on favourable terms and conditions, and on an urgent basis, to *informatique*, to relevant information on advanced and other technologies suited to their specific needs as well as on new uses of existing technology, new developments and possibilities of adapting them to local needs. Inasmuch as in market economies advanced technologies with respect to industrial production are most frequently developed by private institutions, developed countries should facilitate and encourage these institutions in providing effective technologies in support of the priorities of developing countries.

5. Developed countries should give developing countries the freest and fullest possible access to technologies whose transfer is not subject to private decision.

6. Developed countries should improve the transparency of the industrial property market in order to facilitate the technological choices of developing countries. In this respect, relevant organizations of the United Nations system, with the collaboration of developed countries, should undertake projects in the fields of information, consultancy and training for the benefit of developing countries.

7. A United Nations Conference on Science and Technology for Development should be held in 1978 or 1979 with the main objectives of strengthening the technological capacity of developing countries to enable them to apply science and technology to their own development; adopting effective means for the utilization of scientific and technological potentials in the solution of development problems of regional and global significance, especially for the benefit of developing countries; and providing instruments of co-operation to developing countries in the utilization of science and technology for solving socio-economic problems that cannot be solved by individual action, in accordance with national priorities, taking into account the recommendations made by the Intergovernmental Working Group of the Committee on Science and Technology for Development.

8. The United Nations system should play a major role, with appropriate financing, in achieving the above-stated objectives and in developing scientific and technological co-operation between all States in order to ensure the application of science and technology to development. The work of the relevant United Nations bodies, in particular that of the United Nations Conference on Trade and Development, the United Nations Industrial Development Organization, the International Labour Organisation, the United Nations Educational, Scientific and Cultural Organization, the Food and Agriculture Organization of the United Nations, the World Intellectual Property Organization and the United Nations Development Programme, to facilitate the transfer and diffusion of technology should be given urgent priority. The Secretary-General of the United Nations should take steps to ensure that the technology and experience available within the United Nations system is widely disseminated and readily available to the developing countries in need of it.

9. The World Health Organization and the competent organs of the United Nations system, in particular the United Nations Children's Fund, should intensify the international effort aimed at improving health conditions in developing countries by giving

priority to prevention of disease and malnutrition and by providing primary health services to the communities, including maternal and child health and family welfare.

10. Since the outflow of qualified personnel from developing to developed countries seriously hampers the development of the former, there is an urgent need to formulate national and international policies to avoid the "brain drain" and to obviate its adverse effects.

IV. INDUSTRIALIZATION

1. The General Assembly endorses the Lima Declaration and Plan of Action on Industrial Development Co-operation[15] and requests all Governments to take individually and/or collectively the necessary measures and decisions required to implement effectively their undertakings in terms of the Lima Declaration and Plan of Action.

2. Developed countries should facilitate the development of new policies and strengthen existing policies, including labour market policies, which would encourage the redeployment of their industries which are less competitive internationally to developing countries, thus leading to structural adjustments in the former and a higher degree of utilization of natural and human resources in the latter. Such policies may take into account the economic structure and the economic, social and security objectives of the developed countries concerned and the need for such industries to move into more viable lines of production or into other sectors of the economy.

3. A system of consultations as provided for by the Lima Plan of Action should be established at the global, regional, interregional and sectoral levels within the United Nations Industrial Development Organization and within other appropriate international bodies, between developed and developing countries and among developing countries themselves, in order to facilitate the achievement of the goals set forth in the field of industrialization, including the redeployment of certain productive capacities existing in developed countries and the creation of new industrial facilities in developing countries. In this context, the United Nations Industrial Development Organization should serve as a forum for negotiation of agreements in the field of industry between developed and developing countries and among developing countries themselves, at the request of the countries concerned.

4. The Executive Director of the United Nations Industrial Development Organization should take immediate action to ensure the readiness of that organization to serve as a forum for consultations and negotiation of agreements in the field of industry. In reporting to the next session of the Industrial Development Board on actions taken in this respect, the Executive Director should also include proposals for the establishment of a system of consultations. The Industrial Development Board is invited to draw up, at an early date, the rules of procedure according to which this system would operate.

5. To promote co-operation between developed and developing countries, both should endeavour to disseminate appropriate information about their priority areas for industrial co-operation and the form

they would like such co-operation to take. The efforts undertaken by the United Nations Conference on Trade and Development on tripartite co-operation between countries having different economic and social systems could lead to constructive proposals for the industrialization of developing countries.

6. Developed countries should, whenever possible, encourage their enterprises to participate in investment projects within the framework of the development plans and programmes of the developing countries which so desire; such participation should be carried out in accordance with the laws and regulations of the developing countries concerned.

7. A joint study should be undertaken by all Governments under the auspices of the United Nations Industrial Development Organization, in consultation with the Secretary-General of the United Nations Conference on Trade and Development, making full use of the knowledge, experience and capacity existing in the United Nations system of methods and mechanisms for diversified financial and technical co-operation which are geared to the special and changing requirements of international industrial co-operation, as well as of a general set of guidelines for bilateral industrial co-operation. A progress report on this study should be submitted to the General Assembly at its thirty-first session.

8. Special attention should be given to the particular problems in the industrialization of the least developed, land-locked and island developing countries—in order to put at their disposal those technical and financial resources as well as critical goods which need to be provided to them to enable them to overcome their specific problems and to play their due role in the world economy, warranted by their human and material resources.

9. The General Assembly endorses the recommendation of the Second General Conference of the United Nations Industrial Development Organization to convert that organization into a specialized agency and decides to establish a Committee on the Drafting of a Constitution for the United Nations Industrial Development Organization, which shall be an intergovernmental committee of the whole, including States which participated in the Second General Conference, to meet in Vienna to draw up a constitution for the United Nations Industrial Development Organization as a specialized agency, to be submitted to a conference of plenipotentiaries to be convened by the Secretary-General in the last quarter of 1976.

10. In view of the importance of the forthcoming Tripartite World Conference on Employment, Income Distribution, Social Progress and the International Division of Labour, Governments should undertake adequate preparations and consultations.

V. FOOD AND AGRICULTURE

1. The solution to world food problems lies primarily in rapidly increasing food production in the developing countries. To this end, urgent and necessary changes in the pattern of world food production should be introduced and trade policy measures should be implemented, in order to obtain a notable increase in agricultural production and the export earnings of developing countries.

2. To achieve these objectives, it is essential that developed countries, and developing countries in a

[15] See A/10112, chap. IV.

position to do so, should substantially increase the volume of assistance to developing countries for agriculture and food production, and that developed countries should effectively facilitate access to their markets for food and agricultural products of export interest to developing countries, both in raw and processed form, and adopt adjustment measures, where necessary.

3. Developing countries should accord high priority to agricultural and fisheries development, increase investment accordingly and adopt policies which give adequate incentives to agricultural producers. It is a responsibility of each State concerned, in accordance with its sovereign judgement and development plans and policies, to promote interaction between expansion of food production and socioeconomic reforms, with a view to achieving an integrated rural development. The further reduction of post-harvest food losses in developing countries should be undertaken as a matter of priority, with a view to reaching at least a 50 per cent reduction by 1985. All countries and competent international organizations should co-operate financially and technically in the effort to achieve this objective. Particular attention should be given to improvement in the systems of distribution of food-stuffs.

4. The Consultative Group on Food Production and Investment in Developing Countries should quickly identify developing countries having the potential for most rapid and efficient increase of food production, as well as the potential for rapid agricultural expansion in other developing countries, especially the countries with food deficits. Such an assessment would assist developed countries and the competent international organizations to concentrate resources for the rapid increase of agricultural production in the developing countries.

5. Developed countries should adopt policies aimed at ensuring a stable supply and sufficient quantity of fertilizers and other production inputs to developing countries at reasonable prices. They should also provide assistance to, and promote investments in, developing countries to improve the efficiency of their fertilizer and other agricultural input industries. Advantage should be taken of the mechanism provided by the International Fertilizer Supply Scheme.

6. In order to make additional resources available on concessional terms for agricultural development in developing countries, developed countries and developing countries in a position to do so should pledge, on a voluntary basis, substantial contributions to the proposed International Fund for Agricultural Development so as to enable it to come into being by the end of 1975, with initial resources of SDR 1,000 million. Thereafter, additional resources should be provided to the Fund on a continuing basis.

7. In view of the significant impact of basic and applied agricultural research on increasing the quantity and quality of food production, developed countries should support the expansion of the work of the existing international agricultural research centres. Through their bilateral programmes they should strengthen their links with these international research centres and with the national agricultural research centres in developing countries. With respect to the improvement of the productivity and competitiveness with synthetics of non-food agricultural and forestry products, research and technological assistance should be co-ordinated and financed through an appropriate mechanism.

8. In view of the importance of food aid as a transitional measure, all countries should accept both the principle of a minimum food aid target and the concept of forward planning of food aid. The target for the 1975-1976 season should be 10 million tons of food grains. They should also accept the principle that food aid should be channelled on the basis of objective assessment of requirements in the recipient countries. In this respect all countries are urged to participate in the Global Information and Early Warning System on Food and Agriculture.

9. Developed countries should increase the grant component of food aid, where food is not at present provided as grants, and should accept multilateral channelling of these resources at an expanding rate. In providing food grains and financing on soft terms to developing countries in need of such assistance, developed countries and the World Food Programme should take due account of the interests of the food-exporting developing countries and should ensure that such assistance includes, wherever possible, purchases of food from the food-exporting developing countries.

10. Developed countries, and developing countries in a position to do so, should provide food grains and financial assistance on most favourable terms to the most seriously affected countries, to enable them to meet their food and agricultural development requirements within the constraints of their balance-of-payments position. Donor countries should also provide aid on soft terms, in cash and in kind, through bilateral and multilateral channels, to enable the most seriously affected countries to obtain their estimated requirements of about 1 million tons of plant nutrients during 1975-1976.

11. Developed countries should carry out both their bilateral and multilateral food aid channelling in accordance with the procedures of the Principles of Surplus Disposal of the Food and Agriculture Organization of the United Nations so as to avoid causing undue fluctuations in market prices or the disruption of commercial markets for exports of interest to exporting developing countries.

12. All countries should subscribe to the International Undertaking on World Food Security. They should build up and maintain world food-grain reserves, to be held nationally or regionally and strategically located in developed and developing, importing and exporting countries, large enough to cover foreseeable major production shortfalls. Intensive work should be continued on a priority basis in the World Food Council and other appropriate forums in order to determine, *inter alia*, the size of the required reserve, taking into account among other things the proposal made at the current session that the components of wheat and rice in the total reserve should be 30 million tons. The World Food Council should report to the General Assembly on this matter at its thirty-first session. Developed countries should assist developing countries in their efforts to build up and maintain their agreed shares of such reserves. Pending the establishment of the world food-grain reserve, developed countries and developing countries in a position to do so

should earmark stocks and/or funds to be placed at the disposal of the World Food Programme as an emergency reserve to strengthen the capacity of the Programme to deal with crisis situations in developing countries. The aim should be a target of not less than 500,000 tons.

13. Members of the General Assembly reaffirm their full support for the resolutions of the World Food Conference and call upon the World Food Council to monitor the implementation of the provisions under section V of the present resolution and to report to the General Assembly at its thirty-first session.

VI. CO-OPERATION AMONG DEVELOPING COUNTRIES

1. Developed countries and the United Nations system are urged to provide, as and when requested, support and assistance to developing countries in strengthening and enlarging their mutual co-operation at subregional, regional and interregional levels. In this regard, suitable institutional arrangements within the United Nations development system should be made and, when appropriate, strengthened, such as those within the United Nations Conference on Trade and Development, the United Nations Industrial Development Organization and the United Nations Development Programme.

2. The Secretary-General, together with the relevant organizations of the United Nations system, is requested to continue to provide support to ongoing projects and activities, and to commission further studies through institutions in developing countries, which would take into account the material already available within the United Nations system, including in particular the regional commissions and the United Nations Conference on Trade and Development, and in accordance with existing subregional and regional arrangements. These further studies, which should be submitted to the General Assembly at its thirty-first session, should, as a first step, cover:

(*a*) Utilization of know-how, skills, natural resources, technology and funds available within developing countries for promotion of investments in industry, agriculture, transport and communications;

(*b*) Trade liberalization measures including payments and clearing arrangements, covering primary commodities, manufactured goods and services, such as banking, shipping, insurance and reinsurance;

(*c*) Transfer of technology.

3. These studies on co-operation among developing countries, together with other initiatives, would contribute to the evolution towards a system for the economic development of developing countries.

VII. RESTRUCTURING OF THE ECONOMIC AND SOCIAL SECTORS OF THE UNITED NATIONS SYSTEM

1. With a view to initiating the process of restructuring the United Nations system so as to make it more fully capable of dealing with problems of inter-

national economic co-operation and development in a comprehensive and effective manner, in pursuance of General Assembly resolutions 3172 (XXVIII) of 17 December 1973 and 3343 (XXIX) of 17 December 1974, and to make it more responsive to the requirements of the provisions of the Declaration and the Programme of Action on the Establishment of a New International Economic Order as well as those of the Charter of Economic Rights and Duties of States, an *Ad Hoc* Committee on the Restructuring of the Economic and Social Sectors of the United Nations System, which shall be a committee of the whole of the General Assembly open to the participation of all States,[16] is hereby established to prepare detailed action proposals. The *Ad Hoc* Committee should start its work immediately and inform the General Assembly at its thirtieth session on the progress made, and submit its report to the Assembly at its thirty-first session, through the Economic and Social Council at its resumed session. The *Ad Hoc* Committee should take into account in its work, *inter alia*, the relevant proposals and documentation submitted in preparation for the seventh special session of the General Assembly pursuant to Assembly resolution 3343 (XXIX) and other relevant decisions, including the report of the Group of Experts on the Structure of the United Nations System entitled *A New United Nations Structure for Global Economic Co-operation*,[17] the records of the relevant deliberations of the Economic and Social Council, the Trade and Development Board, the Governing Council of the United Nations Development Programme and the seventh special session of the General Assembly, as well as the results of the forthcoming deliberations on institutional arrangements of the United Nations Conference on Trade and Development at its fourth session and of the Governing Council of the United Nations Environment Programme at its fourth session. All United Nations organs, including the regional commissions, as well as the specialized agencies and the International Atomic Energy Agency, are invited to participate at the executive level in the work of the *Ad Hoc* Committee and to respond to requests that the Committee may make to them for information, data or views.

2. The Economic and Social Council should meanwhile continue the process of rationalization and reform which it has undertaken in accordance with Council resolution 1768 (LIV) of 18 May 1973 and General Assembly resolution 3341 (XXIX) of 17 December 1974, and should take into full consideration those recommendations of the *Ad Hoc* Committee that fall within the scope of these resolutions, at the latest at its resumed sixty-first session.

2349th plenary meeting
16 September 1975

---

[16] It is the understanding of the General Assembly that the "all States" formula will be applied in accordance with the established practice of the General Assembly.
[17] E/AC.62/9 (United Nations publication, Sales No. E.75.II.A.7).

FURTHER READINGS

Barraclough, Geoffrey. "The Haves and the Have Nots." *The New York Review of Books,* 23:8, May 13, 1976.

Boserup, Ester, and Christina Liljencrantz. *Integration of Women in Development.* New York: UNDP, 1975.

Brown, Lester R., and Erik P. Eckholm. *By Bread Alone.* New York: Praeger, 1974.

Brown, Lester R., with Patricia L. McGrath and Bruce Stokes. *Twenty-two Dimensions of the Population Problem.* Washington, D.C.: Worldwatch Institute, 1976.

Bundy, William. *The World Economic Crisis.* New York: Norton, 1975.

Cole, John. *The Poor of the Earth.* London: Macmillan, 1976.

Connelly, Philip, and Robert Perlman. *Resource Conflicts in International Relations.* New York: Oxford University Press, 1975.

Eckholm, Erik P. *Losing Ground.* New York: Norton, 1976.

Ehrlich, Paul. *Population Bomb.* New York: Ballantine Books, 1968.

Erb, Guy F., and Valeriana Kallab, ed. *Beyond Dependency.* New York: Praeger, 1975.

Goulet, Dennis. *The Cruel Choice.* New York: Atheneum, 1971.

Heilbroner, Robert. *An Enquiry into the Human Prospect.* New York: Norton, 1974.

McNamara, Robert S. *One Hundred Countries, Two Billion People: The Dimensions of Development.* New York: Praeger, 1973.

Meadows, Donnella M., with Dennis L. Meadows, Jorgen Randers, and William W. Behrens III. *The Limits to Growth.* New York: Universe Books, 1972.

Mesarovic, Mihajlo, and Eduard Pestel. *Mankind at the Turning Point, the Second Report of the Club of Rome.* New York: Dutton, 1974.

Nerfin, Marc. "Assessing the Seventh Special Session of the UN General Assembly." *Development Dialogue,* 1976:1. Uppsala: Dag Hammarskjold Foundation.

———. *Report by Congressional Advisers to the Seventh Special Session of the United Nations.* Washington, D.C.: U.S. Government Printing Office, 1975.

———. *Scanning Our Future, A Report from the NGO Forum on the World Economic Order.* New York: Carnegie Endowment for International Peace, 1976.

128   NEW INTERNATIONAL ECONOMIC ORDER

Pearson, Lester B. *Partners in Development, Report of the Commission on International Development.* New York: Praeger, 1969.

Roche, Douglas. *Justice Not Charity, A New Global Ethic for Canada.* Toronto: McClelland and Stewart, 1976.

Salas, Rafael M. *People: An International Choice.* Oxford: Pergamon Press, 1976.

Schumacher, E. F. *Small Is Beautiful, Economics as if People Mattered.* New York: Harper & Row, 1975.

Sen, Sudhir. *A Richer Harvest.* New York: Maryknoll, 1974.

United Nations. *Assessment of the World Food Situation, Present and Future.* World Food Conference. Rome. November 5–16, 1974, E/CONF.65/B.

――――. *Report of HABITAT: UN Conference on Human Settlements (Vancouver, May 31 to June 11, 1976.* A/CONF.70/15.

――――. *Report of the Second General Conference of the UN Industrial Development Organization,* March 1975. ID/CONF.3/31.

――――. *Report of the UN Conference on Human Settlements, June 1972.* A/CONF.48/14/ Rev.1.

――――. *Report of the World Conference on International Women's Year, June 1975.* E/ CONF.66/34.

――――. *Report of the World Food Conference, Rome, November 1974.* E/5587.

――――. *Report of the World Population Conference, August 1974.* E/CONF.60/19.

――――. *Single Year Population Estimates and Projections, 1950–2000.* ESA/P/WP.56, October 1975.

――――. *Special Session Backgrounders. CESI, 1975.*
1. The International Development Strategy
2. The World Economy
3. Six Paradoxes in the World Economic Situation
4. New Directions in International Trade
5. GATT Multilateral Trade Negotiations
6. Agriculture
7. Transfer of Technology and Trade in Invisibles
8. The International Monetary Situation
9. Aid Flows Between Various Groups of Countries and the Developing Countries

――――. *Transnational Corporations, Measures against Corrupt Practices.* E/5838, June 1976.

――――. *World Economic Survey, 1974.* Docs. E/5665 and E/5681/Rev. 1.

UNCTAD. *Briefing Papers:*
1. Towards an Integrated Commodity Policy, June 1975
2. Transfer of Technology: A Pillar of Development, October 1975
3. Trade in Manufactures and Semi-Manufactures: In Search of Equality, December 1975
4. Strength Out of Unity: Economic Cooperation Among Developing Countries, December 1975
5. Developing Countries and Systems of International Finance and Money, February 1976

————. *Declaration of Dakar, Conference of Developing Countries on Raw Materials, February 1975.* UN doc. E/AC.62/6.

————. *Indexation.* TD/B/563, July 7, 1975.

————. *Major Issues Arising from the Transfer of Technology to Developing Countries, 1975 Study.* TD/B/AC.11/10/Rev.2.

————. *Preparation of a Draft Outline of an International Code of Conduct on Transfer of Technology.* Report by the UNCTAD Secretariat, TD/B/C.6/AC.1/2/Supp.1, March 1975.

————. *Question of the Establishment of a Comprehensive International Trade Organization.* TD/B/535/Add.1, February 20, 1975.

————. *The Role of the Patent System in the Transfer of Technology in Developing Countries.* TD/B/AC.11/19/Rev.1, May 1975.

————. *Technological Dependence: Its Nature, Consequences and Policy Implications.* TD/190, December 1975.

————. *Terms of Trade of Developing Countries.* TD/CD/Misc.60, August 1975.

————. *Towards a New International Economic Order, A Report by a Commonwealth Experts Group.* London: Commonwealth Secretariat, 1975.

————. *Trade in Primary Commodities: Conflict or Cooperation.* Washington, D.C.: Brookings Institution, 1974.

UNESCO. *Moving Towards Change, Some Thoughts on the New International Economic Order.* Paris: UNESCO, 1976.

Victor-Bostrom Fund. *Food and Population.* Report no. 19, 1974. Washington, D.C.: Victor-Bostrom Fund.

Ward, Barbara. *The Home of Man.* New York: Norton, 1976.

————. *Reviewing the International Order, Interim Report.* Rotterdam: Project Rio c/o Bonwcentrum International Education, 1975.

Ward, Barbara, and René Dubos. *Only One Earth.* New York: Ballantine Books, 1973.

ABOUT THE AUTHOR

Jyoti Shankar Singh, who was educated at Banaras, Delhi and London, holds degrees in political science and law. He worked with international voluntary agencies in Asia and Europe before joining the United Nations in 1972. During 1973–74 he was Assistant Executive Secretary of the World Population Year Secretariat, and is now with the United Nations Fund for Population Activities. Singh is a contributing editor of POPULI, and has written extensively on population and development issues in major journals and magazines around the world. He was at the Sixth and Seventh Special Sessions of the UN General Assembly as well as at the UN Conferences on Population (1974), Women (1975), and Human Settlements (1976).